75 Diabetic and Sugar-Free Recipes for Home

By: Kelly Johnson

Table of Contents

Breakfast:
- Vegetable Omelette
- Almond Flour Waffles
- Egg Muffins
- Cottage Cheese and Pineapple Bowl
- Mushroom and Spinach Frittata
- Coconut Chia Seed Smoothie
- Greek Yogurt Parfait
- Chia Seed Pudding
- Blueberry Almond Flour Muffins
- Cinnamon Apple Quinoa Porridge
- Egg White and Vegetable Breakfast Burrito
- Peanut Butter Banana Smoothie
- Sweet Potato and Spinach Breakfast Casserole
- Smoked Salmon Avocado Toast
- Cauliflower Hash Browns

Soups and Salads:
- Chicken and Vegetable Soup
- Roasted Red Pepper and Tomato Soup
- Arugula and Feta Salad with Balsamic Vinaigrette
- Lentil and Vegetable Stew
- Caprese Salad Skewers
- Broccoli and Cheddar Soup
- Cabbage and Sausage Soup
- Shrimp and Avocado Salad
- Asparagus and Almond Salad
- Cauliflower and Broccoli Soup
- Mexican Quinoa Bowl
- Quinoa Salad
- Spinach and Strawberry Salad
- Tomato Basil Soup
- Avocado Chicken Salad

Main Courses:
- Grilled Salmon with Lemon and Herbs
- Grilled Chicken with Rosemary
- Mushroom and Spinach Stuffed Chicken Breast

- Cauliflower Pizza Crust with Vegetables
- Sesame Ginger Baked Tofu
- Turkey and Vegetable Stir-Fry
- Grilled Portobello Mushrooms with Pesto
- Spaghetti Squash with Turkey Bolognese
- Stir-Fried Tofu and Vegetables
- Cajun Shrimp with Zoodles
- Baked Cod with Herbs
- Cauliflower Fried Rice
- Turkey Lettuce Wraps
- Zucchini Noodles with Pesto
- Eggplant Lasagna

Snacks:

- Hummus with Veggies
- Guacamole with Jicama Sticks
- Spicy Roasted Chickpeas
- Cucumber and Cream Cheese Roll-Ups
- Avocado Salsa
- Pistachio Trail Mix
- Cottage Cheese Stuffed Bell Peppers
- Crispy Kale Chips
- Edamame Hummus
- Stuffed Bell Peppers with Cream Cheese
- Greek Yogurt Bark
- Cheese and Nut Platter
- Roasted Chickpeas
- Cucumber Slices with Tzatziki
- Deviled Eggs

Desserts:

- Sugar-Free Apple Crisp
- Almond Butter Cookies
- Sugar-Free Lemon Sorbet
- Pumpkin Pie Chia Pudding
- Raspberry coconut Panna Cotta
- Walnut and Date Energy Balls
- Dark Chocolate Covered Strawberries
- Chocolate Avocado Mousse
- Baked Cinnamon Apple Slices
- Coconut Flour Banana Bread
- Sugar-Free Berry Sorbet

- Almond Joy Energy Bites
- Coconut Flour Pancakes
- Sugar-Free Cheesecake
- Avocado Chocolate Mousse

Breakfast

Vegetable Omelette Recipe

Ingredients:

- 2 large eggs
- 1/4 cup diced bell peppers (assorted colors)
- 1/4 cup diced tomatoes
- 1/4 cup diced onions
- 1/4 cup chopped spinach
- 1 tablespoon olive oil
- Salt and pepper to taste
- Optional: Grated cheese (cheddar, feta, or your preference)

Instructions:

Prepare Vegetables:
- Dice bell peppers, tomatoes, and onions. Chop spinach.

Preheat Pan:
- Heat olive oil in a non-stick skillet over medium heat.

Sauté Vegetables:
- Add diced onions and bell peppers to the pan. Sauté until softened, about 2-3 minutes.

Add Spinach:
- Add chopped spinach to the pan and cook briefly until wilted.

Whisk Eggs:
- In a bowl, whisk the eggs until well beaten. Season with salt and pepper to taste.

Pour Eggs into Pan:
- Pour the beaten eggs over the sautéed vegetables in the pan.

Swirl and Cook:
- Swirl the pan to ensure an even distribution of eggs. Allow the omelette to cook undisturbed for a minute or until the edges start setting.

Add Tomatoes:
- Sprinkle diced tomatoes over one half of the omelette.

Optional Cheese:
- If desired, sprinkle grated cheese over the tomatoes.

Fold and Serve:

- Once the edges are set and the center is slightly runny, carefully fold the omelette in half using a spatula.

Finish Cooking:
- Cook for an additional 1-2 minutes until the eggs are fully cooked but still moist.

Serve Warm:
- Slide the omelette onto a plate, and serve immediately.

Feel free to customize this vegetable omelette by adding your favorite herbs, spices, or other vegetables. It's a versatile and nutritious breakfast option that can be tailored to suit individual preferences.

Almond Flour Waffles Recipe

Ingredients:

- 1 1/2 cups almond flour
- 2 tablespoons coconut flour
- 1 teaspoon baking powder
- 1/4 teaspoon salt
- 3 large eggs
- 1/2 cup almond milk (unsweetened)
- 2 tablespoons melted coconut oil or butter
- 1 tablespoon natural sweetener (e.g., erythritol or stevia), optional
- 1 teaspoon vanilla extract

Instructions:

Preheat Waffle Iron:
- Preheat your waffle iron according to the manufacturer's instructions.

Mix Dry Ingredients:
- In a large bowl, whisk together almond flour, coconut flour, baking powder, and salt.

Whisk Wet Ingredients:
- In a separate bowl, whisk together eggs, almond milk, melted coconut oil (or butter), sweetener (if using), and vanilla extract.

Combine Wet and Dry Ingredients:
- Pour the wet ingredients into the bowl with the dry ingredients. Stir until just combined. The batter should be thick and smooth.

Let Batter Rest:
- Allow the batter to rest for a few minutes. Almond flour can absorb liquids, and the batter may thicken slightly.

Grease Waffle Iron:
- Lightly grease the waffle iron with coconut oil or non-stick cooking spray.

Cook Waffles:
- Pour the batter onto the preheated waffle iron, spreading it evenly. Close the lid and cook until the waffles are golden brown and crisp.

Serve Warm:
- Carefully remove the waffles from the iron and place them on a plate. Serve immediately.

Optional Toppings:

- Top the waffles with fresh berries, a dollop of Greek yogurt, chopped nuts, or a drizzle of sugar-free syrup.

These almond flour waffles are not only delicious but also gluten-free and low in carbohydrates. Adjust the sweetness to your liking, and enjoy a satisfying breakfast treat without added sugars.

Almond Flour Waffles Recipe

Ingredients:

- 1 1/2 cups almond flour
- 2 tablespoons coconut flour
- 1 teaspoon baking powder
- 1/4 teaspoon salt
- 3 large eggs
- 1/2 cup almond milk (unsweetened)
- 2 tablespoons melted coconut oil or butter
- 1 tablespoon natural sweetener (e.g., erythritol or stevia), optional
- 1 teaspoon vanilla extract

Instructions:

Preheat Waffle Iron:
- Preheat your waffle iron according to the manufacturer's instructions.

Mix Dry Ingredients:
- In a large bowl, whisk together almond flour, coconut flour, baking powder, and salt.

Whisk Wet Ingredients:
- In a separate bowl, whisk together eggs, almond milk, melted coconut oil (or butter), sweetener (if using), and vanilla extract.

Combine Wet and Dry Ingredients:
- Pour the wet ingredients into the bowl with the dry ingredients. Stir until just combined. The batter should be thick and smooth.

Let Batter Rest:
- Allow the batter to rest for a few minutes. Almond flour can absorb liquids, and the batter may thicken slightly.

Grease Waffle Iron:
- Lightly grease the waffle iron with coconut oil or non-stick cooking spray.

Cook Waffles:
- Pour the batter onto the preheated waffle iron, spreading it evenly. Close the lid and cook until the waffles are golden brown and crisp.

Serve Warm:
- Carefully remove the waffles from the iron and place them on a plate. Serve immediately.

Optional Toppings:
- Top the waffles with fresh berries, a dollop of Greek yogurt, chopped nuts, or a drizzle of sugar-free syrup.

These almond flour waffles are not only delicious but also gluten-free and low in carbohydrates.

Adjust the sweetness to your liking, and enjoy a satisfying breakfast treat without added sugars.

Egg Muffins Recipe

Ingredients:

- 8 large eggs
- 1/4 cup milk (or a milk substitute)
- 1 cup diced vegetables (bell peppers, spinach, tomatoes, onions, mushrooms, etc.)
- 1/2 cup shredded cheese (cheddar, mozzarella, or your preference)
- Salt and pepper to taste
- Optional: Cooked and crumbled bacon or sausage for added flavor

Instructions:

Preheat Oven:
- Preheat your oven to 350°F (175°C).

Prepare Muffin Tin:
- Grease a muffin tin or use paper liners to prevent sticking.

Whisk Eggs:
- In a large bowl, whisk together the eggs and milk until well combined.

Add Vegetables and Cheese:
- Stir in diced vegetables, shredded cheese, and any optional ingredients (bacon or sausage). Season with salt and pepper.

Fill Muffin Cups:
- Pour the egg mixture evenly into the prepared muffin cups, filling each about 2/3 full.

Bake:
- Bake in the preheated oven for approximately 20-25 minutes or until the egg muffins are set in the center and slightly golden on top.

Cool and Serve:
- Allow the egg muffins to cool in the tin for a few minutes. Use a knife to loosen the edges, and transfer the muffins to a wire rack to cool completely.

Optional Garnish:
- Garnish with additional shredded cheese or fresh herbs if desired.

Serve Warm or Chilled:
- Serve the egg muffins warm, or refrigerate for later. They can be reheated in the microwave for a quick and convenient breakfast.

These egg muffins are versatile, making them an excellent choice for meal prep. You can customize them with your favorite vegetables, cheeses, and protein sources. Enjoy a nutritious and easy-to-make breakfast!

Cottage Cheese and Pineapple Bowl Recipe

Ingredients:
- 1 cup cottage cheese (low-fat or regular)
- 1 cup fresh pineapple chunks (or canned pineapple in juice, drained)
- 1 tablespoon honey (optional)
- 2 tablespoons chopped fresh mint (optional)
- 2 tablespoons chopped nuts (e.g., almonds or walnuts), toasted
- A pinch of cinnamon (optional)

Instructions:

Prepare Ingredients:
- If using fresh pineapple, peel and cut it into bite-sized chunks. If using canned pineapple, make sure to drain the juice.

Combine Cottage Cheese and Pineapple:
- In a mixing bowl, combine the cottage cheese and pineapple chunks.

Drizzle with Honey (Optional):
- If you prefer a sweeter flavor, drizzle honey over the cottage cheese and pineapple. Adjust the amount according to your taste.

Add Mint and Nuts:
- Sprinkle chopped fresh mint and toasted nuts over the cottage cheese and pineapple mixture. This adds a burst of freshness and crunch.

Optional Cinnamon Garnish:
- For an extra layer of flavor, you can sprinkle a pinch of cinnamon on top.

Toss Gently (Optional):
- Gently toss the ingredients to combine evenly, being careful not to break the pineapple chunks.

Serve Immediately:
- Spoon the cottage cheese and pineapple mixture into a serving bowl.

Enjoy:

- Enjoy this simple and nutritious Cottage Cheese and Pineapple Bowl as a refreshing snack or light breakfast.

This recipe is versatile, and you can adjust the ingredients and quantities based on your preferences. It's a delightful combination of creamy cottage cheese, sweet pineapple, and the added crunch of nuts. The touch of honey and mint enhances the overall flavor, making it a delicious and satisfying dish.

Mushroom and Spinach Frittata Recipe

Ingredients:

- 8 large eggs
- 1 cup sliced mushrooms
- 2 cups fresh spinach, chopped
- 1/2 cup diced onions
- 1/2 cup shredded cheese (such as Swiss, cheddar, or feta)
- 2 tablespoons olive oil
- 1 garlic clove, minced
- Salt and pepper to taste
- Fresh herbs for garnish (e.g., parsley or chives)

Instructions:

Preheat Oven:

- Preheat your oven broiler.

Prepare Ingredients:

- Slice mushrooms, chop spinach, dice onions, and shred the cheese.

Sauté Vegetables:

- In an oven-safe skillet, heat olive oil over medium heat. Add diced onions and sliced mushrooms. Sauté until the mushrooms release their moisture and the onions are softened.

Add Garlic and Spinach:

- Add minced garlic to the skillet and sauté for about 30 seconds until fragrant. Add chopped spinach and cook until wilted.

Season with Salt and Pepper:

- Season the vegetable mixture with salt and pepper to taste.

Whisk Eggs:

- In a bowl, whisk the eggs until well beaten. Season with a pinch of salt and pepper.

Pour Eggs into Skillet:

- Pour the beaten eggs over the sautéed vegetables in the skillet. Gently stir to distribute the vegetables evenly.

Cook on Stovetop:

- Allow the frittata to cook on the stovetop over medium heat for a couple of minutes without stirring, allowing the edges to set.

Add Cheese:

- Sprinkle the shredded cheese evenly over the top of the frittata.

Broil in the Oven:

- Transfer the skillet to the preheated oven and broil for 3-5 minutes or until the top is set and slightly golden.

Finish Cooking:

- Keep an eye on the frittata to avoid overcooking. The center should be set but still moist.

Garnish and Serve:

- Remove the skillet from the oven, garnish with fresh herbs, and let it cool for a few minutes. Slice and serve directly from the skillet.

Enjoy this Mushroom and Spinach Frittata as a wholesome breakfast, brunch, or even a light dinner. It's a versatile dish that can be customized with various vegetables and herbs.

Coconut Chia Seed Smoothie Recipe

Ingredients:

- 1 cup coconut milk (unsweetened)
- 1/2 cup coconut water
- 1/2 cup fresh pineapple chunks
- 1/2 banana, frozen
- 2 tablespoons chia seeds
- 1 tablespoon shredded coconut (unsweetened)
- 1 tablespoon lime juice
- 1 teaspoon honey or a natural sweetener (optional)
- Ice cubes (optional)

Instructions:

Prepare Ingredients:

- Measure out all the ingredients.

Soak Chia Seeds:

- In a small bowl, combine chia seeds with coconut water. Let them soak for at least 10-15 minutes, or until they form a gel-like consistency.

Blend Smoothie:

- In a blender, combine coconut milk, pineapple chunks, frozen banana, soaked chia seeds with coconut water, shredded coconut, lime juice, and honey (if using).

Blend Until Smooth:

- Blend the ingredients until smooth. If the smoothie is too thick, you can add more coconut water or coconut milk to achieve your desired consistency.

Adjust Sweetness:

- Taste the smoothie and adjust sweetness, if needed, by adding more honey or your preferred sweetener.

Add Ice Cubes (Optional):

- If you prefer a colder smoothie, add a handful of ice cubes and blend until smooth.

Serve Immediately:

- Pour the Coconut Chia Seed Smoothie into glasses and serve immediately.

Garnish (Optional):

- Garnish with additional shredded coconut or a slice of lime, if desired.

This Coconut Chia Seed Smoothie is not only delicious but also packed with healthy fats, fiber, and tropical flavors. It's a great option for a quick and nutritious breakfast or a refreshing snack. Adjust the ingredients and sweetness to suit your taste preferences. Enjoy!

Greek Yogurt Parfait Recipe

Ingredients:

- 1 cup Greek yogurt (unsweetened)
- 1/2 cup granola (choose a sugar-free or low-sugar option)
- 1/2 cup fresh mixed berries (such as strawberries, blueberries, and raspberries)
- 1 tablespoon honey or maple syrup (optional, depending on sweetness preference)
- 1 tablespoon chopped nuts (e.g., almonds or walnuts)
- A sprinkle of cinnamon (optional)

Instructions:

Prepare Ingredients:

- Measure out the Greek yogurt, granola, mixed berries, honey (if using), and chopped nuts.

Layer Greek Yogurt:

- In a glass or a bowl, start by adding a layer of Greek yogurt at the bottom.

Add Granola Layer:

- Add a layer of granola on top of the Greek yogurt. Ensure an even distribution.

Add Berry Layer:

- Place a layer of mixed berries on top of the granola.

Repeat Layers:

- Repeat the layers until you reach the top of the glass or bowl. You can add as many layers as you prefer.

Drizzle with Honey (Optional):

- If you like your parfait a bit sweeter, drizzle honey or maple syrup over the top.

Sprinkle Nuts and Cinnamon:

- Sprinkle chopped nuts over the parfait for a crunchy texture. Optionally, add a sprinkle of cinnamon for extra flavor.

Serve Immediately:

- Serve the Greek Yogurt Parfait immediately to enjoy the freshness and texture of the layers.

This Greek Yogurt Parfait is a versatile recipe, and you can customize it with different fruits, nuts, and granola varieties. It's a balanced and satisfying option for breakfast, snack, or even a healthy dessert. Adjust the ingredients to suit your taste preferences and dietary needs. Enjoy!

Chia Seed Pudding Recipe

Ingredients:

- 1/4 cup chia seeds
- 1 cup milk of your choice (almond milk, coconut milk, or dairy milk)
- 1-2 tablespoons honey or maple syrup (adjust to taste)
- 1/2 teaspoon vanilla extract
- Fresh fruits or berries for topping (optional)
- Nuts or seeds for garnish (optional)

Instructions:

Combine Chia Seeds and Milk:

- In a bowl or jar, combine the chia seeds, milk, honey or maple syrup, and vanilla extract.

Whisk Thoroughly:

- Whisk the ingredients together until well combined. Make sure there are no clumps of chia seeds.

Let it Sit:

- Cover the bowl or jar and refrigerate the mixture for at least 2 hours or overnight. This allows the chia seeds to absorb the liquid and create a pudding-like consistency.

Stir Occasionally:

- After about 30 minutes in the refrigerator, give the mixture a good stir to prevent the chia seeds from clumping together.

Check Consistency:

- If the mixture is too thick after it has set, you can add a bit more milk and stir until you achieve the desired consistency.

Top with Fruits and Nuts:

- Once the chia seed pudding has set, you can top it with fresh fruits, berries, nuts, or seeds for added texture and flavor.

Serve and Enjoy:

- Spoon the chia seed pudding into serving bowls or jars and enjoy a nutritious and delicious treat!

Variations:

- Experiment with different flavors by adding cocoa powder, cinnamon, or a dash of your favorite spice during the mixing stage.

This Chia Seed Pudding is not only a tasty and satisfying dessert but also a nutritious breakfast option. Feel free to get creative with toppings and flavors to suit your preferences. Enjoy!

Blueberry Almond Flour Muffins Recipe

Ingredients:

- 2 cups almond flour
- 1/2 teaspoon baking soda
- 1/4 teaspoon salt
- 3 large eggs
- 1/4 cup melted coconut oil or butter
- 1/3 cup honey or maple syrup
- 1 teaspoon vanilla extract
- 1 cup fresh or frozen blueberries
- Optional: Sliced almonds for topping

Instructions:

Preheat Oven:

- Preheat your oven to 350°F (175°C). Line a muffin tin with paper liners or grease the muffin cups.

Mix Dry Ingredients:

- In a large bowl, whisk together the almond flour, baking soda, and salt.

Whisk Wet Ingredients:

- In another bowl, whisk the eggs. Add melted coconut oil or butter, honey or maple syrup, and vanilla extract. Mix well.

Combine Wet and Dry Ingredients:

- Pour the wet ingredients into the bowl with the dry ingredients. Stir until just combined. Be careful not to overmix.

Add Blueberries:

- Gently fold in the blueberries into the batter.

Fill Muffin Cups:

- Spoon the batter into the prepared muffin cups, filling each about 2/3 full.

Optional Almond Topping:
- If desired, sprinkle sliced almonds on top of each muffin.

Bake:
- Bake in the preheated oven for 20-25 minutes or until a toothpick inserted into the center comes out clean.

Cool:
- Allow the muffins to cool in the tin for a few minutes, then transfer them to a wire rack to cool completely.

Serve and Enjoy:
- Once cooled, serve these delicious Blueberry Almond Flour Muffins and enjoy!

These muffins are gluten-free, and the almond flour provides a lovely nutty flavor. Feel free to adjust the sweetness by varying the amount of honey or maple syrup, depending on your preference. Enjoy these muffins as a delightful breakfast or a healthy snack!

Cinnamon Apple Quinoa Porridge Recipe

Ingredients:

- 1/2 cup quinoa, rinsed
- 1 cup water
- 1 cup milk (dairy or plant-based)
- 1 large apple, peeled, cored, and diced
- 1-2 tablespoons maple syrup or honey
- 1 teaspoon ground cinnamon
- 1/4 teaspoon nutmeg (optional)
- 1/4 cup chopped nuts (walnuts, almonds, or pecans), toasted
- 1/2 teaspoon vanilla extract
- Pinch of salt
- Greek yogurt or milk for serving (optional)

Instructions:

Rinse Quinoa:

- Rinse quinoa under cold water to remove any bitterness.

Cook Quinoa:

- In a saucepan, combine quinoa and water. Bring to a boil, then reduce heat to low, cover, and simmer for about 15 minutes or until the quinoa is cooked and water is absorbed.

Prepare Apples:

- While the quinoa is cooking, in a separate skillet, sauté diced apples over medium heat with a bit of water until they are tender but not mushy.

Combine Quinoa and Apples:

- Once the quinoa is cooked, add the sautéed apples, milk, maple syrup or honey, ground cinnamon, nutmeg (if using), vanilla extract, and a pinch of salt. Stir well.

Simmer:

- Simmer the mixture over low heat for an additional 5-7 minutes, stirring occasionally until the porridge reaches your desired consistency.

Adjust Sweetness:

- Taste and adjust sweetness if needed by adding more maple syrup or honey.

Serve:

- Spoon the Cinnamon Apple Quinoa Porridge into bowls.

Top with Nuts:

- Top each serving with toasted nuts for added crunch and flavor.

Optional: Serve with Yogurt or Additional Milk:

- Optionally, serve with a dollop of Greek yogurt or an extra splash of milk.

Enjoy Warm:

- Enjoy this cozy Cinnamon Apple Quinoa Porridge while it's warm.

This porridge is not only a hearty and nutritious breakfast but also a delightful way to start your day with the comforting flavors of cinnamon and apples. Feel free to customize the toppings and sweetness to suit your taste preferences!

Egg White and Vegetable Breakfast Burrito Recipe

Ingredients:

- 1 whole wheat or whole grain tortilla
- 1 cup egg whites (or about 4-6 large egg whites)
- 1/4 cup diced bell peppers (assorted colors)
- 1/4 cup diced tomatoes
- 1/4 cup diced onions
- 1/4 cup chopped spinach or kale
- 1 tablespoon olive oil
- Salt and pepper to taste
- Optional toppings: Salsa, avocado slices, shredded cheese, or Greek yogurt

Instructions:

Prepare Vegetables:
- In a skillet, heat olive oil over medium heat. Add diced onions and cook until translucent.

Add Vegetables:
- Add diced bell peppers and chopped spinach or kale to the skillet. Sauté until the vegetables are tender.

Scramble Egg Whites:
- Pour the egg whites into the skillet with the sautéed vegetables. Season with salt and pepper. Cook, stirring occasionally, until the egg whites are fully cooked.

Warm Tortilla:
- In a separate pan or on a griddle, warm the whole wheat or whole grain tortilla.

Assemble the Burrito:
- Place the cooked egg white and vegetable mixture in the center of the tortilla.

Add Optional Toppings:

- Add diced tomatoes and any optional toppings you desire, such as salsa, avocado slices, shredded cheese, or a dollop of Greek yogurt.

Fold and Roll:

- Fold the sides of the tortilla over the filling, then roll it up from the bottom to create a burrito.

Serve Warm:

- Serve the Egg White and Vegetable Breakfast Burrito warm.

This breakfast burrito is not only a great source of protein but also loaded with colorful vegetables, making it a nutritious and satisfying way to start your day. Feel free to customize the ingredients and toppings to suit your taste preferences. Enjoy!

Peanut Butter Banana Smoothie Recipe

Ingredients:

- 1 ripe banana, peeled and sliced
- 1 cup milk (dairy or plant-based)
- 2 tablespoons peanut butter (unsweetened)
- 1 tablespoon honey or maple syrup (optional, depending on sweetness preference)
- 1/2 teaspoon vanilla extract
- 1/2 cup ice cubes
- Optional: A sprinkle of cinnamon or a dash of cocoa powder for extra flavor

Instructions:

Prepare Ingredients:

- Slice the banana and gather all the ingredients.

Combine in Blender:

- In a blender, combine the sliced banana, milk, peanut butter, honey or maple syrup (if using), vanilla extract, and ice cubes.

Blend Until Smooth:

- Blend the ingredients until smooth and creamy. If the smoothie is too thick, you can add more milk to achieve your desired consistency.

Taste and Adjust Sweetness:

- Taste the smoothie and adjust sweetness if needed by adding more honey or maple syrup.

Optional Enhancements:

- Add a sprinkle of cinnamon or a dash of cocoa powder for an extra flavor boost.

Blend Again (Optional):

- If you added any optional enhancements, blend the smoothie again to incorporate the flavors.

Serve Immediately:

- Pour the Peanut Butter Banana Smoothie into a glass and enjoy immediately.

This smoothie is not only delicious but also a great source of protein and healthy fats. It's perfect for a quick and nutritious breakfast or a satisfying snack. Feel free to customize the recipe by adding ingredients like chia seeds, Greek yogurt, or spinach for added nutrients. Enjoy your smoothie!

Sweet Potato and Spinach Breakfast Casserole Recipe

Ingredients:

- 2 medium sweet potatoes, peeled and grated
- 1 cup fresh spinach, chopped
- 8 large eggs
- 1/2 cup milk (dairy or plant-based)
- 1 cup shredded cheddar cheese
- 1 small onion, finely chopped
- 2 cloves garlic, minced
- 1 teaspoon olive oil
- 1 teaspoon dried thyme
- Salt and pepper to taste
- Cooking spray or extra olive oil for greasing the baking dish

Instructions:

Preheat Oven:

- Preheat your oven to 375°F (190°C).

Prepare Sweet Potatoes:

- Peel and grate the sweet potatoes. Place them in a clean kitchen towel and squeeze out any excess moisture.

Sauté Onion and Garlic:

- In a skillet, heat olive oil over medium heat. Add finely chopped onion and minced garlic. Sauté until the onion becomes translucent.

Add Spinach:

- Add chopped spinach to the skillet and cook until wilted. Remove from heat.

Whisk Eggs and Milk:

- In a large bowl, whisk together the eggs and milk until well combined. Season with salt, pepper, and dried thyme.

Combine Ingredients:

- Add the grated sweet potatoes, sautéed spinach mixture, and shredded cheddar cheese to the egg mixture. Mix until everything is evenly combined.

Grease Baking Dish:

- Grease a baking dish with cooking spray or a bit of olive oil.

Pour Mixture into Baking Dish:

- Pour the sweet potato and spinach mixture into the prepared baking dish, spreading it evenly.

Bake:

- Bake in the preheated oven for 30-35 minutes or until the casserole is set and the edges are golden brown.

Cool and Slice:

- Allow the casserole to cool for a few minutes before slicing it into squares or wedges.

Serve Warm:

- Serve the Sweet Potato and Spinach Breakfast Casserole warm.

This casserole is not only delicious but also a nutritious way to start your day with the goodness of sweet potatoes and spinach. Feel free to customize the recipe by adding other vegetables or herbs according to your taste preferences. Enjoy!

Smoked Salmon Avocado Toast Recipe

Ingredients:

- 2 slices of whole-grain bread (or your preferred bread)
- 1 ripe avocado
- 4 oz (about 113g) smoked salmon
- 1 tablespoon cream cheese
- 1 teaspoon capers, drained
- Fresh dill, for garnish
- Lemon wedges, for serving
- Salt and black pepper to taste

Instructions:

Toast the Bread:

- Toast the slices of whole-grain bread to your preferred level of crispiness.

Prepare the Avocado:

- While the bread is toasting, cut the ripe avocado in half, remove the pit, and scoop the flesh into a bowl. Mash the avocado with a fork and season with salt and black pepper to taste.

Spread Avocado on Toast:

- Once the bread is toasted, spread the mashed avocado evenly over each slice.

Add Cream Cheese:

- Dollop cream cheese on top of the mashed avocado, spreading it gently.

Layer with Smoked Salmon:

- Lay slices of smoked salmon over the avocado and cream cheese.

Garnish with Capers and Dill:

- Sprinkle capers over the smoked salmon and garnish with fresh dill.

Serve with Lemon Wedges:

- Serve the Smoked Salmon Avocado Toast with lemon wedges on the side for a bright and citrusy flavor.

Optional Extras:

- Feel free to add extras like red onion slices, microgreens, or a sprinkle of red pepper flakes for additional flavor.

Enjoy:

- Serve immediately and enjoy this delicious and nutritious Smoked Salmon Avocado Toast!

This recipe combines the creaminess of avocado, the richness of smoked salmon, and the freshness of dill to create a delightful breakfast or brunch option. It's not only tasty but also packed with healthy fats and proteins. Adjust the toppings and quantities based on your preferences.

Cauliflower Hash Browns Recipe

Ingredients:

- 1 medium cauliflower head, grated or finely chopped
- 1/4 cup grated Parmesan cheese
- 1/4 cup almond flour or coconut flour
- 1 large egg
- 1/2 teaspoon garlic powder
- 1/2 teaspoon onion powder
- 1/2 teaspoon dried thyme
- Salt and black pepper to taste
- Cooking oil (olive oil, coconut oil, or your preferred oil) for frying

Instructions:

Prepare Cauliflower:

- Wash and thoroughly dry the cauliflower. Remove the leaves and stem, and grate the cauliflower using a box grater or pulse it in a food processor until it resembles rice.

Steam or Microwave Cauliflower:

- Place the grated cauliflower in a microwave-safe bowl and microwave for 4-5 minutes or steam it until it's just tender. Allow it to cool for a few minutes.

Squeeze Out Excess Moisture:

- Use a clean kitchen towel or cheesecloth to squeeze out excess moisture from the cooked cauliflower. This step is crucial to achieve crispy hash browns.

Mix Ingredients:

- In a mixing bowl, combine the squeezed cauliflower, grated Parmesan cheese, almond or coconut flour, egg, garlic powder, onion powder, dried thyme, salt, and black pepper. Mix until well combined.

Shape into Patties:

- Take a portion of the mixture and shape it into a patty or hash brown shape. Repeat with the remaining mixture.

Cook in a Skillet:

- Heat a skillet over medium heat and add cooking oil. Place the cauliflower hash browns in the skillet and cook for 3-4 minutes on each side or until golden brown and crispy.

Transfer to a Plate:

- Once cooked, transfer the cauliflower hash browns to a plate lined with paper towels to absorb any excess oil.

Serve Warm:

- Serve the cauliflower hash browns warm, optionally with your favorite dipping sauce or a dollop of Greek yogurt.

Enjoy these cauliflower hash browns as a delicious and nutritious alternative to traditional hash browns. They're low in carbs, gluten-free, and can be a great addition to your breakfast or brunch menu.

Soups and Salads

Chicken and Vegetable Soup Recipe

Ingredients:

- 1 tablespoon olive oil
- 1 onion, diced
- 2 carrots, peeled and sliced
- 2 celery stalks, sliced
- 3 cloves garlic, minced
- 1 pound (about 450g) boneless, skinless chicken breasts or thighs, diced
- 6 cups chicken broth (homemade or low-sodium store-bought)
- 1 can (14 oz) diced tomatoes, undrained
- 1 cup green beans, trimmed and chopped
- 1 cup corn kernels (fresh, frozen, or canned)
- 1 teaspoon dried thyme
- 1 teaspoon dried oregano
- Salt and black pepper to taste
- 2 cups spinach or kale, chopped
- Fresh parsley for garnish (optional)
- Lemon wedges for serving (optional)

Instructions:

Sauté Vegetables:
- In a large pot or Dutch oven, heat olive oil over medium heat. Add diced onion, sliced carrots, and sliced celery. Sauté until the vegetables are softened, about 5 minutes.

Add Garlic and Chicken:
- Add minced garlic and diced chicken to the pot. Cook until the chicken is browned on all sides.

Pour in Chicken Broth:
- Pour in the chicken broth and bring the mixture to a simmer.

Add Tomatoes and Vegetables:
- Add the diced tomatoes (with their juice), chopped green beans, corn kernels, dried thyme, dried oregano, salt, and black pepper. Stir well.

Simmer:

- Allow the soup to simmer for about 15-20 minutes, or until the vegetables are tender and the chicken is fully cooked.

Add Leafy Greens:
- Stir in the chopped spinach or kale and cook for an additional 2-3 minutes until wilted.

Adjust Seasoning:
- Taste the soup and adjust the seasoning with more salt and pepper if needed.

Serve:
- Ladle the Chicken and Vegetable Soup into bowls. Garnish with fresh parsley if desired. Serve with lemon wedges on the side for a burst of freshness.

Enjoy:
- Enjoy this hearty and nutritious Chicken and Vegetable Soup as a comforting meal.

This soup is not only delicious but also versatile. Feel free to customize it by adding other vegetables or herbs based on your preferences. It's perfect for warming up on a chilly day or for a nourishing meal any time of the year.

Roasted Red Pepper and Tomato Soup Recipe

Ingredients:

- 3 large red bell peppers, halved and seeds removed
- 6 large tomatoes, halved
- 1 onion, peeled and quartered
- 3 cloves garlic, peeled
- 2 tablespoons olive oil
- 4 cups vegetable or chicken broth
- 1 can (14 oz) crushed tomatoes
- 1 teaspoon dried basil
- 1 teaspoon dried oregano
- 1/2 teaspoon dried thyme
- Salt and black pepper to taste
- 1/4 teaspoon red pepper flakes (optional, for heat)
- 1/2 cup heavy cream or coconut cream (optional, for creaminess)
- Fresh basil or parsley for garnish
- Croutons or bread for serving (optional)

Instructions:

Preheat Oven:
- Preheat your oven to 400°F (200°C).

Roast Vegetables:
- Place the red bell peppers, tomatoes, onion, and garlic cloves on a baking sheet. Drizzle with olive oil and toss to coat. Roast in the preheated oven for about 30-40 minutes or until the vegetables are tender and slightly charred.

Peel Red Peppers:
- Once roasted, place the red bell peppers in a bowl and cover with plastic wrap. Allow them to steam for 10 minutes. Peel off the skin and discard.

Blend Roasted Vegetables:
- In a blender or food processor, blend the roasted red peppers, tomatoes, onion, and garlic until smooth. You may need to do this in batches.

Simmer Soup:
- Transfer the blended mixture to a large pot. Add vegetable or chicken broth, crushed tomatoes, dried basil, dried oregano, dried thyme, salt, black pepper, and red pepper flakes (if using). Stir well. Bring the soup to a simmer and let it cook for 15-20 minutes to allow the flavors to meld.

Add Cream (Optional):
- If using cream for added creaminess, stir it into the soup. Adjust the seasoning to taste.

Serve:
- Ladle the Roasted Red Pepper and Tomato Soup into bowls. Garnish with fresh basil or parsley. Optionally, serve with croutons or bread.

Enjoy:
- Enjoy this delicious and comforting Roasted Red Pepper and Tomato Soup!

This soup is rich in flavor, and the roasting process adds a depth of taste. It's perfect for a cozy lunch or dinner, especially during colder months. Adjust the level of spiciness and creaminess to suit your preferences.

Arugula and Feta Salad with Balsamic Vinaigrette Recipe

Ingredients:

For the Salad:

- 6 cups fresh arugula, washed and dried
- 1 cup cherry tomatoes, halved
- 1/2 cup red onion, thinly sliced
- 1/2 cup crumbled feta cheese
- 1/4 cup pine nuts or chopped walnuts, toasted (optional)

For the Balsamic Vinaigrette:

- 1/4 cup balsamic vinegar
- 1/2 cup extra-virgin olive oil
- 1 teaspoon Dijon mustard
- 1 clove garlic, minced
- Salt and black pepper to taste

Instructions:

Prepare Salad Ingredients:
- In a large salad bowl, combine the fresh arugula, cherry tomatoes, sliced red onion, crumbled feta cheese, and toasted pine nuts or chopped walnuts.

Make Balsamic Vinaigrette:
- In a small bowl or jar, whisk together the balsamic vinegar, extra-virgin olive oil, Dijon mustard, minced garlic, salt, and black pepper. Alternatively, you can shake the ingredients together in a jar with a tight-fitting lid.

Dress the Salad:
- Drizzle the balsamic vinaigrette over the salad. Start with a small amount and add more according to your taste preferences.

Toss the Salad:
- Gently toss the salad to ensure all the ingredients are well coated with the vinaigrette.

Serve:
- Transfer the Arugula and Feta Salad to individual plates or a serving platter.

Optional Garnish:

- Optionally, garnish the salad with additional crumbled feta, pine nuts, or chopped fresh herbs.

Enjoy:
- Serve the Arugula and Feta Salad immediately and enjoy this refreshing and flavorful dish!

This salad is a wonderful combination of peppery arugula, tangy feta cheese, and the sweetness of cherry tomatoes, all brought together with a balsamic vinaigrette. It makes for a light and tasty side dish for any meal or a delightful standalone lunch. Adjust the ingredients and dressing quantities to suit your taste preferences.

Lentil and Vegetable Stew Recipe

Ingredients:

- 1 cup dry green or brown lentils, rinsed and drained
- 1 onion, diced
- 3 carrots, peeled and diced
- 3 celery stalks, diced
- 3 cloves garlic, minced
- 1 can (14 oz) diced tomatoes
- 1 sweet potato, peeled and diced
- 1 zucchini, diced
- 1 bell pepper, diced (any color)
- 4 cups vegetable broth
- 1 teaspoon ground cumin
- 1 teaspoon ground coriander
- 1 teaspoon paprika
- 1/2 teaspoon turmeric
- 1/2 teaspoon dried thyme
- Salt and black pepper to taste
- 2 cups spinach or kale, chopped
- 2 tablespoons olive oil
- Fresh parsley for garnish (optional)
- Lemon wedges for serving (optional)

Instructions:

Sauté Vegetables:
- In a large pot or Dutch oven, heat olive oil over medium heat. Add diced onion, carrots, and celery. Sauté until the vegetables are softened.

Add Garlic and Spices:
- Add minced garlic to the pot and sauté for an additional minute. Stir in ground cumin, ground coriander, paprika, turmeric, dried thyme, salt, and black pepper. Cook for another minute to toast the spices.

Add Lentils and Broth:
- Add rinsed lentils, diced tomatoes (with their juice), sweet potato, zucchini, bell pepper, and vegetable broth to the pot. Stir well to combine.

Simmer:

- Bring the stew to a simmer. Reduce heat to low, cover the pot, and let it simmer for about 25-30 minutes or until the lentils and vegetables are tender.

Adjust Seasoning:
- Taste the stew and adjust the seasoning if needed, adding more salt and pepper to taste.

Add Leafy Greens:
- Stir in chopped spinach or kale and cook for an additional 2-3 minutes until the greens are wilted.

Serve:
- Ladle the Lentil and Vegetable Stew into bowls. Garnish with fresh parsley if desired. Serve with lemon wedges on the side for a burst of freshness.

Enjoy:
- Enjoy this wholesome Lentil and Vegetable Stew as a satisfying and nutritious meal!

This stew is not only delicious but also a great source of plant-based protein and fiber. It's perfect for a comforting dinner, and you can customize the vegetables and spices to suit your taste preferences. Serve it with crusty bread or on its own for a complete and wholesome meal.

Caprese Salad Skewers Recipe

Ingredients:

- Fresh cherry tomatoes
- Fresh mozzarella balls (bocconcini)
- Fresh basil leaves
- Balsamic glaze
- Extra-virgin olive oil
- Salt and black pepper to taste
- Wooden or metal skewers

Instructions:

Prepare Ingredients:
- Rinse the cherry tomatoes and pat them dry. Drain the mozzarella balls if they are stored in water.

Assemble Skewers:
- On each skewer, thread a cherry tomato, followed by a fresh basil leaf, and then a mozzarella ball. Repeat until the skewer is filled or until you have the desired number of skewers.

Arrange on Serving Platter:
- Arrange the Caprese Salad Skewers on a serving platter.

Drizzle with Olive Oil and Balsamic Glaze:
- Drizzle extra-virgin olive oil and balsamic glaze over the skewers. The balsamic glaze adds a sweet and tangy flavor to the Caprese Salad.

Season with Salt and Pepper:
- Sprinkle a pinch of salt and black pepper over the skewers to taste.

Serve:
- Serve the Caprese Salad Skewers immediately as a fresh and vibrant appetizer.

Enjoy:
- Enjoy the combination of juicy tomatoes, creamy mozzarella, and aromatic basil in each bite!

This Caprese Salad Skewers recipe is not only visually appealing but also bursting with the classic flavors of a Caprese salad. It's a great option for summer gatherings or any time you want a quick and elegant appetizer. Feel free to customize by adding a drizzle of honey or a sprinkle of chopped fresh herbs for extra flair.

Broccoli and Cheddar Soup Recipe

Ingredients:

- 2 tablespoons butter
- 1 onion, diced
- 2 cloves garlic, minced
- 3 cups fresh broccoli florets, chopped
- 3 cups vegetable or chicken broth
- 1 cup milk (whole or 2%)
- 1/2 cup heavy cream (optional for extra creaminess)
- 2 cups shredded sharp cheddar cheese
- 1/4 cup all-purpose flour
- Salt and black pepper to taste
- 1/4 teaspoon nutmeg (optional)
- Croutons or additional shredded cheddar for garnish (optional)

Instructions:

Sauté Onion and Garlic:
- In a large pot, melt the butter over medium heat. Add diced onions and cook until softened. Add minced garlic and sauté for another 1-2 minutes.

Add Flour:
- Sprinkle flour over the sautéed onions and garlic. Stir well to create a roux. Cook for 2-3 minutes to eliminate the raw flour taste.

Add Broccoli:
- Add chopped broccoli florets to the pot. Stir to coat the broccoli with the roux.

Pour in Broth:
- Pour in the vegetable or chicken broth, stirring constantly. Bring the mixture to a simmer.

Simmer Until Broccoli is Tender:
- Allow the soup to simmer for about 15-20 minutes or until the broccoli is tender.

Blend (Optional):
- For a smoother consistency, you can use an immersion blender to partially blend the soup, leaving some chunks of broccoli intact. Alternatively, transfer a portion of the soup to a blender, blend, and return it to the pot.

Add Milk and Cream:
- Pour in the milk and heavy cream (if using). Stir to combine.

Add Cheddar Cheese:
- Gradually add the shredded cheddar cheese, stirring continuously until the cheese is melted and the soup is creamy.

Season:
- Season the soup with salt, black pepper, and nutmeg (if using). Adjust the seasoning to your taste.

Serve:
- Ladle the Broccoli and Cheddar Soup into bowls. Optionally, garnish with croutons or additional shredded cheddar.

Enjoy:
- Serve the soup hot and enjoy the comforting flavors of Broccoli and Cheddar!

This rich and creamy soup is a classic favorite, combining the goodness of broccoli with the rich and savory taste of cheddar cheese. It's perfect for a cozy meal, especially during colder weather. Adjust the thickness and seasonings according to your preference.

Cabbage and Sausage Soup Recipe

Ingredients:

- 1 lb (450g) smoked sausage, sliced
- 1 tablespoon olive oil
- 1 onion, diced
- 3 cloves garlic, minced
- 1 small head of cabbage, chopped
- 3 carrots, peeled and sliced
- 3 potatoes, peeled and diced
- 8 cups chicken or vegetable broth
- 1 can (14 oz) diced tomatoes, undrained
- 1 teaspoon dried thyme
- 1 teaspoon dried oregano
- 1 bay leaf
- Salt and black pepper to taste
- Fresh parsley for garnish (optional)

Instructions:

Brown Sausage:
- In a large pot, heat olive oil over medium heat. Add the sliced smoked sausage and brown it for 3-4 minutes until it gets a bit crispy. Remove some of the sausage slices for later garnish if desired.

Sauté Onion and Garlic:
- Add diced onion and minced garlic to the pot. Sauté until the onion is translucent.

Add Vegetables:
- Add chopped cabbage, sliced carrots, and diced potatoes to the pot. Stir well to combine.

Pour in Broth and Tomatoes:
- Pour in the chicken or vegetable broth and add the diced tomatoes with their juice. Stir in dried thyme, dried oregano, bay leaf, salt, and black pepper.

Simmer:
- Bring the soup to a simmer. Cover and let it simmer for about 20-25 minutes or until the vegetables are tender.

Adjust Seasoning:

- Taste the soup and adjust the seasoning with more salt and pepper if needed.

Serve:
- Ladle the Cabbage and Sausage Soup into bowls. Garnish with the reserved crispy sausage slices and fresh parsley if desired.

Enjoy:
- Serve the soup hot and enjoy the hearty and comforting flavors!

This Cabbage and Sausage Soup is a wholesome and filling dish, perfect for a satisfying meal. It's easy to make and can be customized with your favorite herbs and spices. Feel free to experiment with the ingredients and adjust the quantities to suit your taste preferences.

Shrimp and Avocado Salad Recipe

Ingredients:

For the Shrimp:

- 1 lb (about 450g) large shrimp, peeled and deveined
- 1 tablespoon olive oil
- 1 teaspoon smoked paprika
- Salt and black pepper to taste
- 1 clove garlic, minced (optional)

For the Salad:

- 4 cups mixed salad greens (lettuce, spinach, arugula, etc.)
- 2 ripe avocados, peeled, pitted, and sliced
- 1 cup cherry tomatoes, halved
- 1 cucumber, sliced
- 1/4 red onion, thinly sliced

For the Dressing:

- 3 tablespoons extra-virgin olive oil
- 2 tablespoons fresh lemon juice
- 1 teaspoon Dijon mustard
- 1 clove garlic, minced
- Salt and black pepper to taste

Instructions:

Prepare Shrimp:
- In a bowl, toss the peeled and deveined shrimp with olive oil, smoked paprika, salt, pepper, and minced garlic. Let it marinate for about 15 minutes.

Cook Shrimp:
- Heat a skillet over medium-high heat. Add the marinated shrimp and cook for 2-3 minutes on each side or until they turn pink and opaque. Be careful not to overcook.

Make Dressing:

- In a small bowl, whisk together extra-virgin olive oil, fresh lemon juice, Dijon mustard, minced garlic, salt, and black pepper to make the dressing.

Assemble Salad:
- In a large salad bowl or individual plates, arrange the mixed salad greens. Top with sliced avocados, cherry tomatoes, cucumber, and thinly sliced red onion.

Add Cooked Shrimp:
- Place the cooked shrimp on top of the salad.

Drizzle with Dressing:
- Drizzle the dressing over the salad, ensuring even coverage.

Toss Gently:
- Gently toss the salad to combine all the ingredients and coat them with the dressing.

Serve:
- Serve the Shrimp and Avocado Salad immediately.

Enjoy:
- Enjoy this light and flavorful salad as a refreshing meal or appetizer.

This Shrimp and Avocado Salad is not only delicious but also a great source of protein, healthy fats, and fresh veggies. It's perfect for a quick and satisfying lunch or dinner. Feel free to customize the salad with additional herbs, nuts, or your favorite salad toppings.

Asparagus and Almond Salad Recipe

Ingredients:

- 1 bunch of fresh asparagus, tough ends trimmed
- 2 tablespoons olive oil
- Salt and black pepper to taste
- 1/2 cup slivered almonds, toasted
- Zest of 1 lemon
- 2 tablespoons fresh lemon juice
- 2 tablespoons extra-virgin olive oil
- 1 teaspoon Dijon mustard
- 1 clove garlic, minced
- 1 tablespoon honey or maple syrup (optional, for sweetness)
- 4 cups mixed salad greens (arugula, spinach, or your choice)
- 1/4 cup crumbled feta cheese (optional)
- Lemon wedges for serving

Instructions:

Preheat Oven:
- Preheat your oven to 400°F (200°C).

Roast Asparagus:
- Place trimmed asparagus on a baking sheet. Drizzle with 2 tablespoons of olive oil, and season with salt and black pepper. Toss to coat evenly. Roast in the preheated oven for about 10-12 minutes or until the asparagus is tender yet still crisp.

Toast Almonds:
- In a dry skillet over medium heat, toast the slivered almonds until they are golden brown. Keep an eye on them as they can burn quickly. Set aside.

Make Dressing:
- In a small bowl, whisk together lemon zest, lemon juice, extra-virgin olive oil, Dijon mustard, minced garlic, and honey or maple syrup (if using). Season with salt and black pepper to taste.

Assemble Salad:
- In a large salad bowl, arrange the mixed salad greens. Top with the roasted asparagus.

Drizzle with Dressing:
- Drizzle the lemon-Dijon dressing over the salad.

Add Almonds:

- Sprinkle the toasted slivered almonds over the salad.

Optional Feta Cheese:
- If desired, crumble feta cheese over the top for added creaminess.

Toss Gently:
- Gently toss the salad to coat the ingredients with the dressing.

Serve:
- Serve the Asparagus and Almond Salad immediately, garnished with lemon wedges on the side.

Enjoy:
- Enjoy this light and flavorful salad as a side dish or a refreshing main course.

This Asparagus and Almond Salad is not only delicious but also packed with vibrant flavors and textures. The combination of roasted asparagus, toasted almonds, and a zesty lemon-Dijon dressing creates a delightful dish. Adjust the sweetness of the dressing according to your preference.

Cauliflower and Broccoli Soup Recipe

Ingredients:

- 1 tablespoon olive oil
- 1 onion, chopped
- 2 cloves garlic, minced
- 1 head cauliflower, chopped into florets
- 1 broccoli crown, chopped into florets
- 4 cups vegetable broth
- 1 teaspoon dried thyme
- 1 teaspoon dried rosemary
- Salt and black pepper to taste
- 1 cup unsweetened almond milk or regular milk
- 1/2 cup heavy cream (optional, for added creaminess)
- 1/2 cup shredded cheddar cheese (optional, for extra flavor)
- Chopped chives or parsley for garnish

Instructions:

Sauté Onion and Garlic:
- In a large pot, heat olive oil over medium heat. Add chopped onion and sauté until softened. Add minced garlic and cook for an additional minute.

Add Cauliflower and Broccoli:
- Add the cauliflower and broccoli florets to the pot. Stir well to coat them with the onion and garlic.

Pour in Broth:
- Pour in the vegetable broth, ensuring that the cauliflower and broccoli are mostly covered. Add dried thyme, dried rosemary, salt, and black pepper. Stir to combine.

Simmer Until Tender:
- Bring the mixture to a simmer, then reduce the heat to low. Cover and let it simmer for about 15-20 minutes or until the cauliflower and broccoli are tender.

Blend Soup:
- Use an immersion blender to blend the soup until smooth. Alternatively, transfer the soup to a blender in batches, blend, and return it to the pot.

Add Milk and Cream:
- Stir in the almond milk or regular milk. If you want a creamier soup, add the heavy cream. Mix well.

Adjust Seasoning:
- Taste the soup and adjust the seasoning, adding more salt and pepper if needed.

Optional Cheese:
- If desired, stir in shredded cheddar cheese until melted, adding extra flavor to the soup.

Serve:
- Ladle the Cauliflower and Broccoli Soup into bowls.

Garnish:
- Garnish with chopped chives or parsley.

Enjoy:
- Serve the soup hot and enjoy the comforting flavors of Cauliflower and Broccoli!

This soup is a delicious way to enjoy the goodness of cauliflower and broccoli in a warm and creamy bowl. Adjust the consistency and seasonings according to your preference. It's perfect for a cozy meal on a chilly day.

Mexican Quinoa Bowl Recipe

Ingredients:

For the Quinoa:

- 1 cup quinoa, rinsed and drained
- 2 cups vegetable broth or water
- 1 teaspoon ground cumin
- 1 teaspoon chili powder
- 1/2 teaspoon garlic powder
- Salt and black pepper to taste

For the Bowl:

- 1 tablespoon olive oil
- 1 onion, diced
- 1 bell pepper, diced (any color)
- 1 cup corn kernels (fresh, frozen, or canned)
- 1 can (15 oz) black beans, drained and rinsed
- 1 cup cherry tomatoes, halved
- 1 avocado, sliced
- Fresh cilantro, chopped, for garnish
- Lime wedges, for serving

For the Dressing:

- 3 tablespoons lime juice
- 2 tablespoons olive oil
- 1 teaspoon honey or agave syrup
- Salt and black pepper to taste

Instructions:

Cook Quinoa:
- In a medium saucepan, combine quinoa, vegetable broth or water, ground cumin, chili powder, garlic powder, salt, and black pepper. Bring to a boil, then reduce the heat, cover, and simmer for 15-20 minutes or until the quinoa is cooked and the liquid is absorbed. Fluff the quinoa with a fork.

Prepare Vegetables:

- In a large skillet, heat olive oil over medium heat. Add diced onion and bell pepper. Sauté until softened. Add corn kernels and black beans. Cook for an additional 3-4 minutes until everything is heated through.

Make Dressing:
- In a small bowl, whisk together lime juice, olive oil, honey or agave syrup, salt, and black pepper.

Assemble Bowls:
- Divide the cooked quinoa among serving bowls. Top with the sautéed vegetable mixture.

Add Fresh Toppings:
- Add cherry tomatoes, sliced avocado, and any additional toppings you like.

Drizzle with Dressing:
- Drizzle the lime dressing over the bowls.

Garnish:
- Garnish with chopped fresh cilantro.

Serve:
- Serve the Mexican Quinoa Bowls with lime wedges on the side.

Enjoy:
- Enjoy this flavorful and nutritious Mexican Quinoa Bowl!

This bowl is not only colorful and vibrant but also packed with protein and wholesome ingredients. Customize it with your favorite toppings like shredded cheese, salsa, or sour cream. It's a perfect dish for a quick and satisfying meal.

Quinoa Salad Recipe

Ingredients:

For the Quinoa:

- 1 cup quinoa, rinsed and drained
- 2 cups water or vegetable broth
- 1/2 teaspoon salt

For the Salad:

- 1 cucumber, diced
- 1 red bell pepper, diced
- 1 yellow bell pepper, diced
- 1 cup cherry tomatoes, halved
- 1/4 cup red onion, finely chopped
- 1/4 cup Kalamata olives, pitted and sliced
- 1/4 cup crumbled feta cheese (optional)

For the Dressing:

- 3 tablespoons extra-virgin olive oil
- 2 tablespoons red wine vinegar
- 1 teaspoon Dijon mustard
- 1 clove garlic, minced
- Salt and black pepper to taste
- Fresh herbs like parsley or basil, chopped (optional)

Instructions:

Cook Quinoa:

- In a medium saucepan, combine quinoa, water or vegetable broth, and salt. Bring to a boil, then reduce the heat to low, cover, and simmer for 15-20 minutes or until the quinoa is cooked and the liquid is absorbed. Fluff the quinoa with a fork and let it cool.

Prepare Vegetables:

- In a large bowl, combine the diced cucumber, red and yellow bell peppers, cherry tomatoes, red onion, and Kalamata olives.

Make Dressing:

- In a small bowl, whisk together the olive oil, red wine vinegar, Dijon mustard, minced garlic, salt, and black pepper.

Assemble Salad:

- Add the cooked and cooled quinoa to the bowl with the vegetables.

Add Dressing:

- Drizzle the dressing over the quinoa and vegetables.

Toss Gently:

- Gently toss the salad to combine all the ingredients and coat them with the dressing.

Optional Feta Cheese:

- If using, sprinkle crumbled feta cheese over the top of the salad.

Garnish:

- Garnish with fresh herbs like parsley or basil, if desired.

Chill (Optional):

- Refrigerate the quinoa salad for at least 30 minutes before serving to allow the flavors to meld.

Serve:

- Serve the Quinoa Salad as a refreshing side dish or a light and nutritious main course.

Enjoy:

- Enjoy this versatile and healthy Quinoa Salad!

Feel free to customize this salad by adding your favorite vegetables, nuts, or protein sources. It's perfect for a quick and satisfying meal, and it can be enjoyed on its own or as a side dish.

Spinach and Strawberry Salad Recipe

Ingredients:

For the Salad:

- 6 cups fresh baby spinach, washed and dried
- 2 cups strawberries, hulled and sliced
- 1/2 cup red onion, thinly sliced
- 1/2 cup crumbled feta cheese or goat cheese
- 1/4 cup sliced almonds or candied pecans, toasted

For the Dressing:

- 3 tablespoons balsamic vinegar
- 2 tablespoons extra-virgin olive oil
- 1 tablespoon honey or maple syrup
- 1 teaspoon Dijon mustard
- Salt and black pepper to taste

Instructions:

Prepare Salad Ingredients:

- In a large salad bowl, combine the fresh baby spinach, sliced strawberries, thinly sliced red onion, crumbled feta cheese, and toasted sliced almonds or candied pecans.

Make Dressing:

- In a small bowl, whisk together balsamic vinegar, extra-virgin olive oil, honey or maple syrup, Dijon mustard, salt, and black pepper. Adjust the sweetness and acidity according to your taste.

Drizzle Dressing:

- Drizzle the dressing over the salad ingredients.

Toss Gently:

- Gently toss the salad to coat the ingredients evenly with the dressing.

Serve:

- Serve the Spinach and Strawberry Salad immediately.

Enjoy:

- Enjoy this refreshing and flavorful salad as a light meal or a side dish!

This Spinach and Strawberry Salad combines the sweetness of strawberries with the earthy flavor of spinach, creating a delicious and vibrant dish. The feta cheese adds a creamy texture, and the nuts provide a satisfying crunch. It's a perfect salad for spring and summer, and you can customize it by adding grilled chicken or avocado if desired.

Tomato Basil Soup Recipe

Ingredients:

- 2 tablespoons olive oil
- 1 onion, chopped
- 2 cloves garlic, minced
- 1 can (28 oz) whole peeled tomatoes
- 1 can (14 oz) diced tomatoes
- 1 teaspoon sugar (optional, to balance acidity)
- 1 cup vegetable broth
- 1/2 cup heavy cream (optional, for creaminess)
- Salt and black pepper to taste
- 1/2 cup fresh basil leaves, chopped
- Grated Parmesan cheese for garnish (optional)
- Croutons or bread for serving (optional)

Instructions:

Sauté Onion and Garlic:

- In a large pot, heat olive oil over medium heat. Add chopped onion and sauté until softened. Add minced garlic and cook for an additional minute.

Add Tomatoes:

- Pour in both cans of tomatoes (with their juices). Break apart the whole tomatoes using a spoon. Stir in sugar if using.

Simmer:

- Add vegetable broth, salt, and black pepper. Bring the mixture to a simmer. Cover and let it simmer for about 20-25 minutes, allowing the flavors to meld.

Blend Soup:

- Use an immersion blender to carefully blend the soup until smooth. Alternatively, transfer the soup to a blender in batches, blend, and return it to the pot.

Add Cream (Optional):

- Stir in heavy cream if you want a creamier consistency. Adjust the seasoning to taste.

Add Basil:

- Add chopped fresh basil to the soup. Stir well.

Simmer Briefly:

- Let the soup simmer for an additional 5 minutes to allow the basil flavor to infuse.

Serve:

- Ladle the Tomato Basil Soup into bowls.

Garnish:

- Garnish with grated Parmesan cheese if desired. Serve with croutons or bread on the side.

Enjoy:

- Enjoy this comforting and flavorful Tomato Basil Soup!

This Tomato Basil Soup is perfect for a cozy and satisfying meal. The combination of ripe tomatoes and fresh basil creates a deliciously rich and aromatic flavor. Adjust the creaminess and seasonings according to your taste preferences. Serve it with a side of crusty bread for a complete experience.

Avocado Chicken Salad Recipe

Ingredients:

- 2 cups cooked chicken breast, shredded or diced
- 2 ripe avocados, peeled, pitted, and diced
- 1 cup cherry tomatoes, halved
- 1/4 cup red onion, finely chopped
- 1/4 cup fresh cilantro, chopped
- Juice of 1 lime
- 2 tablespoons extra-virgin olive oil
- Salt and black pepper to taste
- Lettuce leaves or bread for serving (optional)

Instructions:

Prepare Chicken:

- Cook chicken breast by boiling, grilling, or baking. Shred or dice the cooked chicken into bite-sized pieces.

Dice Avocados:

- In a large mixing bowl, dice the ripe avocados.

Combine Ingredients:

- Add the shredded or diced chicken to the bowl with avocados. Add halved cherry tomatoes, finely chopped red onion, and fresh cilantro.

Prepare Dressing:

- In a small bowl, whisk together the lime juice, extra-virgin olive oil, salt, and black pepper.

Drizzle Dressing:

- Drizzle the dressing over the chicken and avocado mixture.

Toss Gently:
- Gently toss the ingredients until everything is well coated with the dressing.

Adjust Seasoning:
- Taste the salad and adjust the seasoning, adding more salt and pepper if needed.

Chill (Optional):
- Refrigerate the Avocado Chicken Salad for about 30 minutes to allow the flavors to meld.

Serve:
- Serve the salad on a bed of lettuce leaves, in a sandwich, or with your favorite bread.

Enjoy:
- Enjoy this refreshing and creamy Avocado Chicken Salad!

This Avocado Chicken Salad is a perfect combination of creamy avocados, tender chicken, and fresh vegetables. It can be served as a light and satisfying lunch, a refreshing dinner, or as a filling for sandwiches or wraps. Feel free to customize with additional ingredients like bell peppers, corn, or your favorite herbs.

Main Courses

Grilled Salmon with Lemon and Herbs Recipe

Ingredients:

- 4 salmon fillets
- 2 tablespoons olive oil
- 2 tablespoons fresh lemon juice
- Zest of 1 lemon
- 2 cloves garlic, minced
- 1 tablespoon fresh parsley, chopped
- 1 tablespoon fresh dill, chopped
- Salt and black pepper to taste
- Lemon wedges for serving

Instructions:

    Prepare the Marinade:

- In a bowl, whisk together olive oil, fresh lemon juice, lemon zest, minced garlic, chopped parsley, chopped dill, salt, and black pepper.

    Marinate the Salmon:

- Place the salmon fillets in a shallow dish or a resealable plastic bag. Pour the marinade over the salmon, ensuring each fillet is well coated. Allow it to marinate for at least 30 minutes in the refrigerator.

    Preheat the Grill:

- Preheat your grill to medium-high heat.

    Prepare Salmon for Grilling:

- Remove the salmon from the refrigerator and let it come to room temperature for about 10 minutes. This helps ensure even cooking.

Grill the Salmon:

- Grease the grill grates to prevent sticking. Place the salmon fillets on the preheated grill, skin-side down. Grill for about 4-5 minutes per side or until the salmon easily flakes with a fork.

Baste with Marinade (Optional):

- Optionally, you can baste the salmon with some of the remaining marinade while grilling for added flavor.

Check for Doneness:

- The salmon is done when it easily flakes with a fork. Be careful not to overcook to keep it moist and tender.

Serve:

- Transfer the grilled salmon to a serving platter. Garnish with additional fresh herbs and lemon wedges.

Enjoy:

- Serve the Grilled Salmon with Lemon and Herbs hot, and enjoy the delicious flavors!

This Grilled Salmon with Lemon and Herbs is not only flavorful but also quick and easy to prepare. The combination of fresh herbs and zesty lemon enhances the natural taste of the salmon. It's a perfect dish for a light and healthy meal.

Grilled Chicken with Rosemary Recipe

Ingredients:

- 4 boneless, skinless chicken breasts
- 3 tablespoons olive oil
- 2 tablespoons fresh rosemary, chopped
- 3 cloves garlic, minced
- Zest of 1 lemon
- Juice of 1 lemon
- Salt and black pepper to taste
- Lemon wedges for serving

Instructions:

Prepare Marinade:

- In a bowl, combine olive oil, chopped fresh rosemary, minced garlic, lemon zest, lemon juice, salt, and black pepper. Mix well to create the marinade.

Marinate Chicken:

- Place the chicken breasts in a shallow dish or a resealable plastic bag. Pour the marinade over the chicken, ensuring each breast is well coated. Allow it to marinate in the refrigerator for at least 30 minutes, or for a more intense flavor, marinate for a few hours or overnight.

Preheat the Grill:

- Preheat your grill to medium-high heat.

Prepare Chicken for Grilling:

- Remove the chicken from the refrigerator and let it come to room temperature for about 10-15 minutes. This helps ensure even cooking.

Grill the Chicken:

- Grease the grill grates to prevent sticking. Place the marinated chicken breasts on the preheated grill. Grill for approximately 6-8 minutes per side or until the internal temperature reaches 165°F (74°C) and the chicken is no longer pink in the center.

Baste with Marinade (Optional):

- Optionally, you can baste the chicken with some of the remaining marinade while grilling for added flavor.

Check for Doneness:

- Use a meat thermometer to ensure the chicken is fully cooked. The juices should run clear, and the internal temperature should reach 165°F (74°C).

Rest and Serve:

- Allow the grilled chicken to rest for a few minutes before serving. This helps the juices redistribute throughout the meat, keeping it moist.

Serve:

- Serve the Grilled Chicken with Rosemary hot, garnished with additional fresh rosemary and lemon wedges.

Enjoy:

- Enjoy this simple and aromatic Grilled Chicken with Rosemary!

This grilled chicken recipe with rosemary is not only easy to make but also adds a wonderful herbal flavor to the chicken. It's a versatile dish that pairs well with various side dishes or can be sliced and added to salads. The lemon and rosemary combination adds a bright and refreshing touch.

Mushroom and Spinach Stuffed Chicken Breast Recipe

Ingredients:

For the Stuffed Chicken Breast:

- 4 boneless, skinless chicken breasts
- Salt and black pepper to taste
- 1 tablespoon olive oil

For the Mushroom and Spinach Filling:

- 2 cups mushrooms, finely chopped
- 2 cups fresh spinach, chopped
- 3 cloves garlic, minced
- 1 tablespoon olive oil
- Salt and black pepper to taste
- 1/2 cup shredded mozzarella cheese
- 1/4 cup grated Parmesan cheese

For the Garlic Herb Butter:

- 4 tablespoons unsalted butter, melted
- 2 cloves garlic, minced
- 1 teaspoon dried thyme
- 1 teaspoon dried rosemary
- Salt to taste

Instructions:

    Preheat Oven:

- Preheat your oven to 375°F (190°C).

Prepare Chicken Breasts:

- Place each chicken breast between plastic wrap and use a meat mallet to pound them to an even thickness. Season both sides with salt and black pepper.

Make Filling:

- In a skillet, heat 1 tablespoon of olive oil over medium heat. Add minced garlic and chopped mushrooms. Sauté until the mushrooms release their moisture and become tender. Add chopped spinach and cook until wilted. Season with salt and black pepper. Remove from heat and let it cool slightly.

Create Pocket in Chicken:

- Slice a pocket into the thickest side of each chicken breast. Be careful not to cut all the way through.

Stuff Chicken:

- Stuff each chicken breast with the mushroom and spinach mixture. Divide the shredded mozzarella and grated Parmesan cheese among the chicken breasts, stuffing them along with the vegetables.

Secure with Toothpicks:

- Use toothpicks to secure the chicken breasts, closing the pockets and keeping the stuffing inside.

Season and Sear:

- Season the outside of the stuffed chicken breasts with a little salt and black pepper. In an oven-safe skillet, heat 1 tablespoon of olive oil over medium-high heat. Sear the stuffed chicken breasts for about 2 minutes per side, or until golden brown.

Make Garlic Herb Butter:

- In a small bowl, mix melted butter, minced garlic, dried thyme, dried rosemary, and salt.

Baste and Bake:

- Baste the seared chicken breasts with the garlic herb butter. Transfer the skillet to the preheated oven and bake for about 20-25 minutes, or until the chicken is cooked through.

Check Doneness:

- Ensure the internal temperature of the chicken reaches 165°F (74°C).

Rest and Serve:

- Allow the stuffed chicken breasts to rest for a few minutes before serving. Remove toothpicks before serving.

Enjoy:

- Serve the Mushroom and Spinach Stuffed Chicken Breast hot, drizzled with any remaining garlic herb butter.

This Mushroom and Spinach Stuffed Chicken Breast is a flavorful and elegant dish that makes for a delicious main course. The combination of mushrooms, spinach, and melted cheese creates a savory filling, and the garlic herb butter adds a delightful aroma. It's perfect for a special dinner or when you want to impress with a tasty, homemade dish.

Cauliflower Pizza Crust with Vegetables Recipe

Ingredients:

For the Cauliflower Pizza Crust:

- 1 medium-sized cauliflower head, riced (about 4 cups)
- 1/2 cup mozzarella cheese, shredded
- 1/4 cup Parmesan cheese, grated
- 1 large egg
- 1 teaspoon dried oregano
- 1 teaspoon dried basil
- 1/2 teaspoon garlic powder
- Salt and black pepper to taste

For the Pizza Toppings:

- 1/2 cup pizza sauce
- 1 cup mozzarella cheese, shredded
- Assorted vegetables (e.g., bell peppers, cherry tomatoes, red onion, mushrooms), sliced
- Fresh basil or parsley for garnish (optional)
- Red pepper flakes for a spicy kick (optional)

Instructions:

Preheat Oven:

- Preheat your oven to 425°F (220°C). Place a pizza stone or a baking sheet in the oven to heat.

Prepare Cauliflower Rice:

- Cut the cauliflower into florets and pulse in a food processor until it resembles rice.

Steam Cauliflower Rice:

- Place the riced cauliflower in a microwave-safe bowl and microwave for 5-6 minutes or until tender. Alternatively, you can steam it on the stovetop.

Drain and Cool:

- Allow the steamed cauliflower rice to cool slightly. Place it in a clean kitchen towel or cheesecloth and squeeze out as much liquid as possible.

Make Cauliflower Pizza Dough:

- In a bowl, combine the drained cauliflower rice, mozzarella cheese, Parmesan cheese, egg, dried oregano, dried basil, garlic powder, salt, and black pepper. Mix well to form a dough.

Shape Pizza Crust:

- Place the cauliflower dough on a parchment paper-lined surface. Use your hands to flatten and shape it into a round pizza crust, about 1/4-inch thick.

Bake Crust:

- Carefully transfer the parchment paper with the crust onto the preheated pizza stone or baking sheet. Bake for 12-15 minutes or until the crust is golden brown and holds together.

Add Toppings:

- Remove the crust from the oven and spread pizza sauce evenly over the surface. Sprinkle with mozzarella cheese and add sliced vegetables of your choice.

Bake Again:

- Return the pizza to the oven and bake for an additional 10-12 minutes, or until the cheese is melted and bubbly.

Garnish and Serve:

- Remove the cauliflower pizza from the oven. Garnish with fresh basil or parsley and red pepper flakes if desired.

Slice and Enjoy:

- Allow the pizza to cool for a few minutes, then slice and enjoy your Cauliflower Pizza Crust with Vegetables!

This cauliflower pizza crust is a low-carb and gluten-free alternative to traditional pizza crusts. It's a great way to sneak in extra veggies, and you can customize the toppings to suit your taste. Feel free to experiment with different vegetables, cheeses, and herbs to create your favorite cauliflower pizza combination.

Sesame Ginger Baked Tofu Recipe

Ingredients:

For the Marinade:

- 1/4 cup soy sauce (or tamari for a gluten-free option)
- 2 tablespoons sesame oil
- 2 tablespoons rice vinegar
- 1 tablespoon fresh ginger, grated
- 2 cloves garlic, minced
- 1 tablespoon maple syrup or agave nectar
- 1 tablespoon sesame seeds (plus extra for garnish)
- Pinch of red pepper flakes (optional for spice)

For the Baked Tofu:

- 1 block extra-firm tofu, pressed and cubed
- 1 tablespoon cornstarch or arrowroot powder (optional for extra crispiness)

Instructions:

Prepare Marinade:

- In a bowl, whisk together soy sauce, sesame oil, rice vinegar, grated ginger, minced garlic, maple syrup or agave nectar, sesame seeds, and red pepper flakes (if using).

Press Tofu:

- Press the block of tofu to remove excess water. You can do this by wrapping the tofu block in a clean kitchen towel and placing a heavy object (like a cast-iron skillet) on top for about 15-20 minutes.

Preheat Oven:
- Preheat your oven to 400°F (200°C). Line a baking sheet with parchment paper.

Cut Tofu:
- Cut the pressed tofu into cubes of your desired size.

Marinate Tofu:
- Place the tofu cubes in a shallow dish and pour the marinade over them, ensuring all the tofu is well coated. Marinate for at least 15-20 minutes, or longer for more flavor. Optionally, toss the tofu with cornstarch or arrowroot powder for extra crispiness.

Bake Tofu:
- Place the marinated tofu cubes on the prepared baking sheet, leaving space between each piece. Bake in the preheated oven for 25-30 minutes, flipping the tofu halfway through, or until the tofu is golden brown and has a slightly crispy exterior.

Garnish and Serve:
- Remove the baked tofu from the oven and sprinkle with additional sesame seeds for garnish.

Serve:
- Serve the Sesame Ginger Baked Tofu over rice, quinoa, or your favorite salad. Drizzle with any remaining marinade for extra flavor.

Enjoy:
- Enjoy the Sesame Ginger Baked Tofu as a flavorful and protein-packed dish!

This Sesame Ginger Baked Tofu is a tasty and versatile plant-based dish. The marinade gives the tofu a rich umami flavor with a hint of sweetness and warmth from the ginger. It's great as a protein source in bowls, salads, wraps, or on its own. Feel free to customize the recipe by adding your favorite vegetables or sauces.

Turkey and Vegetable Stir-Fry Recipe

Ingredients:

For the Stir-Fry Sauce:

- 3 tablespoons soy sauce
- 2 tablespoons oyster sauce
- 1 tablespoon hoisin sauce
- 1 tablespoon rice vinegar
- 1 tablespoon cornstarch
- 1 tablespoon water
- 1 teaspoon sesame oil

For the Stir-Fry:

- 1 pound ground turkey
- 2 tablespoons vegetable oil, divided
- 3 cloves garlic, minced
- 1 tablespoon fresh ginger, grated
- 1 medium onion, thinly sliced
- 1 bell pepper, thinly sliced (any color)
- 1 medium carrot, julienned
- 1 cup broccoli florets
- 1 cup snap peas, ends trimmed
- 2 green onions, chopped (for garnish)
- Sesame seeds for garnish (optional)
- Cooked rice or noodles for serving

Instructions:

Prepare the Stir-Fry Sauce:
- In a bowl, whisk together soy sauce, oyster sauce, hoisin sauce, rice vinegar, cornstarch, water, and sesame oil. Set aside.

Cook Turkey:
- In a wok or large skillet, heat 1 tablespoon of vegetable oil over medium-high heat. Add the ground turkey and cook, breaking it apart with a spoon, until browned and cooked through. Remove excess fat if needed.

Set Aside Turkey:
- Transfer the cooked turkey to a plate and set aside.

Stir-Fry Vegetables:
- In the same wok or skillet, add another tablespoon of vegetable oil. Add minced garlic and grated ginger, and stir-fry for about 30 seconds until fragrant.

Add Vegetables:
- Add sliced onion, bell pepper, julienned carrot, broccoli florets, and snap peas to the wok. Stir-fry for 3-4 minutes or until the vegetables are crisp-tender.

Combine Turkey and Vegetables:
- Return the cooked turkey to the wok with the stir-fried vegetables.

Pour Sauce:
- Pour the prepared stir-fry sauce over the turkey and vegetables. Toss everything together until well coated and heated through.

Check Seasoning:
- Taste and adjust the seasoning if necessary.

Serve:

- Serve the Turkey and Vegetable Stir-Fry over cooked rice or noodles.

Garnish:

- Garnish with chopped green onions and sesame seeds if desired.

Enjoy:

- Enjoy this delicious and quick Turkey and Vegetable Stir-Fry!

This stir-fry is a perfect balance of flavors and textures, combining the savory turkey with a variety of colorful and crunchy vegetables. Feel free to customize the vegetables based on your preferences. It's a versatile dish that's both nutritious and satisfying.

Grilled Portobello Mushrooms with Pesto Recipe

Ingredients:

For the Grilled Portobello Mushrooms:

- 4 large Portobello mushrooms, stems removed
- 2 tablespoons balsamic vinegar
- 2 tablespoons olive oil
- Salt and black pepper to taste

For the Pesto:

- 2 cups fresh basil leaves, packed
- 1/2 cup grated Parmesan cheese
- 1/2 cup pine nuts or walnuts
- 3 cloves garlic, peeled
- 1/2 cup extra-virgin olive oil
- Salt and black pepper to taste
- Juice of 1 lemon (optional, for added freshness)

Instructions:

Prepare the Portobello Mushrooms:

- Clean the Portobello mushrooms using a damp cloth or a mushroom brush to remove any dirt. Remove the stems.

Marinate Mushrooms:

- In a bowl, whisk together balsamic vinegar, olive oil, salt, and black pepper. Brush the marinade over both sides of the Portobello mushrooms.

Preheat Grill:

- Preheat your grill or grill pan to medium-high heat.

Grill Mushrooms:

- Place the marinated Portobello mushrooms on the preheated grill. Grill for about 4-5 minutes per side, or until the mushrooms are tender and have nice grill marks.

Make Pesto:

- In a food processor, combine fresh basil, grated Parmesan cheese, pine nuts or walnuts, and peeled garlic cloves. Pulse until finely chopped.

Stream in Olive Oil:

- With the food processor running, slowly stream in the extra-virgin olive oil until the pesto reaches your desired consistency. Season with salt and black pepper. Add lemon juice if using.

Check Seasoning:

- Taste the pesto and adjust the seasoning if needed.

Serve:

- Place the grilled Portobello mushrooms on a serving plate. Spoon the freshly made pesto over the top.

Garnish (Optional):

- Garnish with additional grated Parmesan cheese and fresh basil leaves if desired.

Enjoy:

- Serve the Grilled Portobello Mushrooms with Pesto as a delicious appetizer or a side dish.

These Grilled Portobello Mushrooms with Pesto are a delightful and flavorful dish. The earthy taste of the grilled mushrooms pairs wonderfully with the vibrant and herbaceous pesto. It's a great vegetarian option that can be served as an appetizer, side dish, or even as a main course.

Spaghetti Squash with Turkey Bolognese Recipe

Ingredients:

For the Spaghetti Squash:

- 2 medium-sized spaghetti squashes
- Olive oil
- Salt and black pepper to taste

For the Turkey Bolognese Sauce:

- 1 pound ground turkey
- 1 tablespoon olive oil
- 1 onion, finely chopped
- 2 carrots, peeled and finely chopped
- 2 celery stalks, finely chopped
- 3 cloves garlic, minced
- 1 can (28 oz) crushed tomatoes
- 1/2 cup red wine (optional)
- 1 teaspoon dried oregano
- 1 teaspoon dried basil
- 1/2 teaspoon dried thyme
- Salt and black pepper to taste
- 1/4 cup fresh parsley, chopped (for garnish)
- Grated Parmesan cheese (for serving)

Instructions:

    Prepare Spaghetti Squash:

- Preheat your oven to 400°F (200°C).
- Cut the spaghetti squashes in half lengthwise. Scoop out the seeds.
- Brush the cut sides with olive oil and sprinkle with salt and black pepper.
- Place the squash halves, cut side down, on a baking sheet.
- Roast in the preheated oven for 35-45 minutes, or until the squash is tender and easily pierced with a fork.
- Once cooked, use a fork to scrape the squash into spaghetti-like strands.

Make Turkey Bolognese Sauce:

- In a large skillet, heat 1 tablespoon of olive oil over medium heat.
- Add chopped onion, carrots, celery, and garlic. Sauté until the vegetables are softened.

Cook Turkey:

- Add ground turkey to the skillet and cook until browned.

Add Tomatoes and Wine:

- Pour in crushed tomatoes and red wine (if using). Stir to combine.

Season:

- Add dried oregano, dried basil, dried thyme, salt, and black pepper. Stir well.

Simmer:

- Reduce the heat and let the sauce simmer for 20-30 minutes to allow the flavors to meld. Stir occasionally.

Check Seasoning:

- Taste the Bolognese sauce and adjust the seasoning if needed.

Serve:

- Spoon the turkey Bolognese sauce over the roasted spaghetti squash.

Garnish:

- Garnish with fresh parsley and serve with grated Parmesan cheese on the side.

Enjoy:
- Enjoy this wholesome and low-carb Spaghetti Squash with Turkey Bolognese!

This dish provides a healthier alternative to traditional pasta by using spaghetti squash. The turkey Bolognese sauce adds a flavorful and protein-packed element. It's a satisfying and nutritious meal that's perfect for those looking to reduce their carb intake or include more vegetables in their diet.

Stir-Fried Tofu and Vegetables Recipe

Ingredients:

For the Tofu:

- 1 block extra-firm tofu, pressed and cubed
- 2 tablespoons soy sauce
- 1 tablespoon sesame oil
- 1 tablespoon cornstarch

For the Stir-Fry Sauce:

- 3 tablespoons soy sauce
- 2 tablespoons hoisin sauce
- 1 tablespoon rice vinegar
- 1 tablespoon maple syrup or agave nectar
- 1 tablespoon cornstarch
- 1/2 cup vegetable broth or water

For the Stir-Fry:

- 2 tablespoons vegetable oil
- 3 cloves garlic, minced
- 1 tablespoon fresh ginger, grated
- 1 bell pepper, thinly sliced
- 1 carrot, julienned
- 1 cup broccoli florets
- 1 cup snap peas, ends trimmed

- 1 cup mushrooms, sliced
- Green onions, chopped (for garnish)
- Sesame seeds (for garnish)
- Cooked rice or noodles for serving

Instructions:

Prepare Tofu:

- Press the block of tofu to remove excess water. Cut it into cubes.
- In a bowl, toss the tofu cubes with soy sauce, sesame oil, and cornstarch until evenly coated.

Make Stir-Fry Sauce:

- In a small bowl, whisk together soy sauce, hoisin sauce, rice vinegar, maple syrup or agave nectar, cornstarch, and vegetable broth or water. Set aside.

Stir-Fry Tofu:

- In a wok or large skillet, heat 1 tablespoon of vegetable oil over medium-high heat. Add the marinated tofu cubes and stir-fry until they are golden brown and crispy. Remove the tofu from the pan and set aside.

Stir-Fry Vegetables:

- In the same pan, add another tablespoon of vegetable oil. Add minced garlic and grated ginger. Stir-fry for about 30 seconds until fragrant.
- Add sliced bell pepper, julienned carrot, broccoli florets, snap peas, and mushrooms. Stir-fry for 3-4 minutes until the vegetables are crisp-tender.

Combine Tofu and Vegetables:

- Return the cooked tofu to the pan with the stir-fried vegetables. Mix well.

Add Stir-Fry Sauce:

- Pour the prepared stir-fry sauce over the tofu and vegetables. Toss everything together until well coated and heated through.

Check Seasoning:

- Taste and adjust the seasoning if necessary.

Serve:

- Serve the Stir-Fried Tofu and Vegetables over cooked rice or noodles.

Garnish:

- Garnish with chopped green onions and sesame seeds.

Enjoy:

- Enjoy this flavorful and colorful Stir-Fried Tofu and Vegetables!

This stir-fry is a versatile and quick-to-make dish that's perfect for a satisfying and healthy meal. The combination of tofu and a variety of colorful vegetables makes it both delicious and nutritious. Feel free to customize the vegetables based on your preferences, and you can serve it over rice or noodles for a complete and filling meal.

Cajun Shrimp with Zoodles Recipe

Ingredients:

For the Cajun Shrimp:

- 1 pound large shrimp, peeled and deveined
- 2 tablespoons Cajun seasoning
- 2 tablespoons olive oil
- 2 cloves garlic, minced
- Juice of 1 lemon
- Salt and black pepper to taste
- Fresh parsley, chopped (for garnish)

For the Zoodles:

- 4 medium-sized zucchini, spiralized into noodles
- 1 tablespoon olive oil
- Salt and black pepper to taste

Instructions:

Marinate Shrimp:

- In a bowl, toss the peeled and deveined shrimp with Cajun seasoning, minced garlic, olive oil, lemon juice, salt, and black pepper. Let it marinate for about 15-20 minutes.

Prepare Zoodles:

- Spiralize the zucchini into noodles using a spiralizer.

Cook Shrimp:

- In a large skillet, heat olive oil over medium-high heat. Add the marinated shrimp to the skillet and cook for 2-3 minutes on each side or until the shrimp are opaque and cooked through.

Remove Shrimp:

- Once the shrimp are cooked, remove them from the skillet and set aside.

Cook Zoodles:

- In the same skillet, add a bit more olive oil if needed. Add the spiralized zucchini noodles and sauté for 2-3 minutes, or until the zoodles are just tender but still have a bit of crunch.

Combine Shrimp and Zoodles:

- Add the cooked shrimp back to the skillet with the zoodles. Toss everything together until well combined and heated through.

Check Seasoning:

- Taste and adjust the seasoning if necessary.

Garnish:

- Garnish with chopped fresh parsley.

Serve:

- Serve the Cajun Shrimp with Zoodles immediately, either on its own or over a bed of mixed greens.

Enjoy:

- Enjoy this light, flavorful, and low-carb Cajun Shrimp with Zoodles!

This dish is not only delicious but also a healthier alternative to traditional pasta. The Cajun seasoning adds a bold and spicy flavor to the shrimp, and the zoodles provide a refreshing and nutritious base. It's a quick and easy meal that's perfect for a satisfying lunch or dinner.

Baked Cod with Herbs Recipe

Ingredients:

- 4 cod fillets (about 6 ounces each)
- 2 tablespoons olive oil
- 2 tablespoons fresh lemon juice
- 2 cloves garlic, minced
- 1 teaspoon dried oregano
- 1 teaspoon dried thyme
- 1 teaspoon dried rosemary
- Salt and black pepper to taste
- Lemon wedges for serving
- Fresh parsley, chopped (for garnish)

Instructions:

Preheat Oven:

- Preheat your oven to 400°F (200°C). Line a baking sheet with parchment paper or lightly grease it.

Prepare Cod Fillets:

- Pat the cod fillets dry with paper towels. Place them on the prepared baking sheet.

Make Herb Marinade:

- In a small bowl, whisk together olive oil, fresh lemon juice, minced garlic, dried oregano, dried thyme, dried rosemary, salt, and black pepper.

Marinate Cod:

- Brush the herb marinade over the cod fillets, ensuring they are well coated on all sides.

Bake Cod:

- Bake in the preheated oven for 12-15 minutes, or until the cod is opaque and flakes easily with a fork.

Broil (Optional):

- If you prefer a golden-brown crust, you can broil the cod for an additional 1-2 minutes at the end of the cooking time. Keep a close eye to prevent burning.

Check Doneness:

- The cod is done when it reaches an internal temperature of 145°F (63°C) and easily flakes with a fork.

Garnish and Serve:

- Transfer the baked cod to serving plates. Garnish with chopped fresh parsley and serve with lemon wedges on the side.

Enjoy:

- Enjoy this Baked Cod with Herbs as a light and flavorful main dish!

This baked cod recipe is a quick and healthy option for a satisfying meal. The combination of herbs and lemon adds a burst of freshness to the mild flavor of the cod. Serve it with your favorite side dishes, such as roasted vegetables or a light salad, for a complete and delicious dinner.

Cauliflower Fried Rice Recipe

Ingredients:

- 1 medium-sized cauliflower, grated or processed into rice-like texture
- 2 tablespoons sesame oil
- 2 cloves garlic, minced
- 1 tablespoon fresh ginger, grated
- 1 cup mixed vegetables (e.g., peas, carrots, corn, diced bell peppers)
- 2 eggs, beaten
- 3 tablespoons soy sauce (or tamari for a gluten-free option)
- 1 tablespoon oyster sauce (optional)
- 2 green onions, chopped
- Salt and black pepper to taste
- Sesame seeds for garnish (optional)

Instructions:

Prepare Cauliflower Rice:

- Grate the cauliflower using a box grater or pulse it in a food processor until it resembles rice. Set aside.

Cook Vegetables:

- In a large wok or skillet, heat sesame oil over medium-high heat. Add minced garlic and grated ginger. Stir-fry for about 30 seconds until fragrant.
- Add mixed vegetables to the wok and stir-fry until they are tender-crisp.

Push Vegetables to the Side:

- Push the cooked vegetables to one side of the wok, creating a clear space.

Cook Eggs:

- Pour the beaten eggs into the clear space in the wok. Allow them to set slightly, and then scramble with a spatula until fully cooked.

Combine Cauliflower Rice:

- Add the grated cauliflower rice to the wok, combining it with the cooked vegetables and eggs.

Season with Sauce:

- Pour soy sauce and oyster sauce (if using) over the cauliflower rice mixture. Stir well to combine and evenly distribute the sauces.

Check Seasoning:

- Taste the cauliflower fried rice and adjust the seasoning with salt and black pepper if needed.

Finish with Green Onions:

- Add chopped green onions to the wok and toss everything together. Cook for an additional 2-3 minutes until the cauliflower rice is heated through.

Garnish:

- Garnish with sesame seeds if desired.

Serve:

- Serve the Cauliflower Fried Rice hot as a delicious and healthy alternative to traditional fried rice.

Enjoy:

- Enjoy this low-carb and veggie-packed Cauliflower Fried Rice as a satisfying main dish or a side!

This Cauliflower Fried Rice is a flavorful and nutritious option that's quick to prepare. The cauliflower rice absorbs the savory flavors of the soy sauce and oyster sauce while providing a light and fluffy texture. Feel free to customize the vegetables to your liking, and you can add cooked protein like chicken, shrimp, or tofu for additional protein.

Turkey Lettuce Wraps Recipe

Ingredients:

For the Turkey Filling:

- 1 pound ground turkey
- 1 tablespoon olive oil
- 1 onion, finely chopped
- 2 cloves garlic, minced
- 1 tablespoon ginger, minced
- 1 red bell pepper, finely diced
- 1 carrot, shredded
- 1/4 cup hoisin sauce
- 2 tablespoons soy sauce (or tamari for a gluten-free option)
- 1 tablespoon rice vinegar
- 1 teaspoon sesame oil
- 2 green onions, chopped
- Salt and black pepper to taste

For Serving:

- Large iceberg or butter lettuce leaves, washed and dried
- Fresh cilantro leaves, chopped
- Sesame seeds (optional)
- Lime wedges

Instructions:

Cook Turkey Filling:

- In a large skillet or wok, heat olive oil over medium-high heat. Add chopped onions and sauté until softened.

Add Aromatics:

- Add minced garlic and minced ginger to the skillet. Stir-fry for about 30 seconds until fragrant.

Cook Ground Turkey:

- Add ground turkey to the skillet and cook until browned, breaking it apart with a spoon as it cooks.

Add Vegetables:

- Stir in diced red bell pepper and shredded carrot. Cook for 2-3 minutes until the vegetables are slightly softened.

Make Sauce:

- In a small bowl, mix hoisin sauce, soy sauce, rice vinegar, sesame oil, salt, and black pepper.

Combine Sauce with Turkey Mixture:

- Pour the sauce over the turkey mixture in the skillet. Stir to combine, ensuring the turkey is evenly coated with the sauce.

Cook and Thicken:

- Cook for an additional 2-3 minutes until the sauce has thickened slightly.

Add Green Onions:

- Stir in chopped green onions and cook for an additional minute.

Check Seasoning:

- Taste the turkey filling and adjust the seasoning if needed.

Prepare Lettuce Leaves:

- Carefully separate and wash large lettuce leaves. Pat them dry with paper towels.

Assemble Lettuce Wraps:

- Spoon the turkey filling into the center of each lettuce leaf.

Garnish and Serve:

- Garnish with chopped cilantro, sesame seeds (if using), and serve with lime wedges on the side.

Enjoy:

- Enjoy these Turkey Lettuce Wraps as a light and flavorful meal!

These Turkey Lettuce Wraps are a great combination of savory, sweet, and crunchy. The crisp lettuce leaves provide a refreshing alternative to traditional wraps, making them a perfect option for a light lunch or dinner. Customize the fillings to suit your taste, and feel free to add additional toppings like chopped peanuts or a drizzle of Sriracha for extra flavor.

Zucchini Noodles with Pesto Recipe

Ingredients:

For the Pesto:

- 2 cups fresh basil leaves, packed
- 1/2 cup grated Parmesan cheese
- 1/2 cup pine nuts or walnuts
- 2 cloves garlic, peeled
- 1/2 cup extra-virgin olive oil
- Salt and black pepper to taste
- Juice of 1 lemon (optional, for added freshness)

For the Zucchini Noodles:

- 4 medium-sized zucchini, spiralized into noodles
- 2 tablespoons olive oil
- Salt and black pepper to taste
- Cherry tomatoes, halved (optional, for garnish)
- Extra Parmesan cheese for serving

Instructions:

Make Pesto:

- In a food processor, combine fresh basil, grated Parmesan cheese, pine nuts or walnuts, and peeled garlic cloves. Pulse until finely chopped.

Stream in Olive Oil:

- With the food processor running, slowly stream in the extra-virgin olive oil until the pesto reaches your desired consistency. Season with salt and black pepper. Add lemon juice if using.

Check Seasoning:

- Taste the pesto and adjust the seasoning if needed. Set aside.

Prepare Zucchini Noodles:

- Spiralize the zucchini into noodles using a spiralizer.

Cook Zucchini Noodles:

- In a large skillet, heat olive oil over medium-high heat. Add the spiralized zucchini noodles and sauté for 2-3 minutes, or until the zoodles are just tender but still have a bit of crunch.

Add Pesto:

- Add the prepared pesto to the skillet with the zucchini noodles. Toss everything together until well coated.

Check Seasoning:

- Taste and adjust the seasoning with salt and black pepper if needed.

Garnish:

- Garnish with halved cherry tomatoes and extra Parmesan cheese if desired.

Serve:

- Serve the Zucchini Noodles with Pesto immediately as a fresh and flavorful dish.

Enjoy:

- Enjoy this light and low-carb Zucchini Noodles with Pesto as a nutritious and satisfying meal!

This dish is a great way to enjoy a lighter alternative to traditional pasta. The pesto adds a burst of flavor to the zucchini noodles, creating a vibrant and delicious dish. It's quick to prepare and makes a perfect lunch or dinner option, especially during warmer months.

Eggplant Lasagna Recipe

Ingredients:

For the Eggplant Layers:

- 2 large eggplants, sliced lengthwise into 1/4-inch thick slices
- Olive oil for brushing
- Salt and black pepper to taste

For the Meat Sauce:

- 1 pound ground beef or turkey
- 1 onion, finely chopped
- 3 cloves garlic, minced
- 1 can (28 oz) crushed tomatoes
- 1 can (6 oz) tomato paste
- 1 teaspoon dried oregano
- 1 teaspoon dried basil
- 1/2 teaspoon dried thyme
- Salt and black pepper to taste

For the Cheese Filling:

- 2 cups ricotta cheese
- 1 cup shredded mozzarella cheese
- 1/2 cup grated Parmesan cheese
- 1 large egg
- 2 tablespoons fresh basil, chopped

- Salt and black pepper to taste

Instructions:

Prepare Eggplant:

- Preheat the oven to 375°F (190°C).
- Slice the eggplants lengthwise into 1/4-inch thick slices. Place the slices on a baking sheet, brush both sides with olive oil, and sprinkle with salt and black pepper.
- Roast in the preheated oven for about 15-20 minutes or until the eggplant slices are softened. Remove from the oven and set aside.

Make Meat Sauce:

- In a large skillet, cook ground beef or turkey over medium heat until browned. Drain excess fat if necessary.
- Add chopped onion and minced garlic to the skillet. Sauté until the onion is softened.
- Stir in crushed tomatoes, tomato paste, dried oregano, dried basil, dried thyme, salt, and black pepper. Simmer for 15-20 minutes, stirring occasionally.

Prepare Cheese Filling:

- In a bowl, combine ricotta cheese, shredded mozzarella cheese, grated Parmesan cheese, egg, chopped fresh basil, salt, and black pepper. Mix well.

Assemble the Lasagna:

- In a baking dish, spread a thin layer of the meat sauce.
- Place a layer of roasted eggplant slices on top of the sauce.
- Spoon half of the ricotta cheese mixture over the eggplant layer.

- Repeat the layers, finishing with a layer of meat sauce on top.

Bake:
- Cover the baking dish with foil and bake in the preheated oven for 25-30 minutes.
- Remove the foil and bake for an additional 10-15 minutes or until the top is golden and bubbly.

Let it Rest:
- Allow the eggplant lasagna to rest for 10-15 minutes before slicing.

Serve:
- Slice, serve, and enjoy your Eggplant Lasagna!

This Eggplant Lasagna is a delicious and satisfying alternative to traditional lasagna. The roasted eggplant layers replace traditional pasta sheets, making it a low-carb option. The combination of flavorful meat sauce and cheesy filling creates a hearty and comforting dish.

Snacks

Hummus with Veggies Recipe

Ingredients:

For the Hummus:

- 1 can (15 oz) chickpeas (garbanzo beans), drained and rinsed
- 1/4 cup tahini
- 1/4 cup extra-virgin olive oil
- 2 tablespoons lemon juice (about 1 lemon)
- 2 cloves garlic, minced
- 1/2 teaspoon ground cumin
- Salt to taste
- 2-3 tablespoons water (as needed for consistency)

For the Veggies:

- Carrot sticks
- Cucumber slices
- Bell pepper strips (assorted colors)
- Cherry tomatoes, halved
- Celery sticks
- Broccoli florets

Instructions:

    Make Hummus:

- In a food processor, combine chickpeas, tahini, olive oil, lemon juice, minced garlic, ground cumin, and a pinch of salt.
- Process until smooth, scraping down the sides as needed.

Adjust Consistency:

- If the hummus is too thick, add water, one tablespoon at a time, until you achieve your desired consistency.

Check Seasoning:

- Taste the hummus and adjust the seasoning by adding more salt or lemon juice if needed.

Prepare Veggies:

- Wash and cut a variety of fresh vegetables into sticks or slices.

Serve:

- Transfer the hummus to a serving bowl. Arrange the vegetable sticks around the hummus.

Garnish (Optional):

- Drizzle a little extra-virgin olive oil over the hummus. Garnish with a sprinkle of paprika or a few chopped fresh herbs, such as parsley.

Enjoy:

- Enjoy the Hummus with Veggies as a healthy and satisfying snack or appetizer!

This combination is not only delicious but also packed with nutrients. The creamy and flavorful hummus pairs perfectly with the crisp and refreshing vegetables. It's a great dish for entertaining or a quick and healthy snack. Feel free to customize the vegetables based on your preferences.

Guacamole with Jicama Sticks Recipe

Ingredients:

For the Guacamole:

- 3 ripe avocados
- 1 medium tomato, diced
- 1/4 cup red onion, finely chopped
- 1/4 cup fresh cilantro, chopped
- 1-2 cloves garlic, minced
- Juice of 1 lime
- Salt and black pepper to taste
- Optional: Jalapeño, finely chopped (for added heat)

For the Jicama Sticks:

- 1 large jicama, peeled and cut into sticks

Instructions:

Prepare Jicama Sticks:

- Peel the jicama and cut it into thin sticks. Set aside.

Make Guacamole:

- In a bowl, mash the ripe avocados with a fork or potato masher until smooth but still slightly chunky.
- Add diced tomato, finely chopped red onion, chopped cilantro, minced garlic, and lime juice to the mashed avocados.
- If you like some heat, add finely chopped jalapeño.
- Season the guacamole with salt and black pepper to taste.

- Gently fold all the ingredients together until well combined.

Serve:

- Transfer the guacamole to a serving bowl.

Garnish (Optional):

- Garnish with additional cilantro or a few tomato and onion pieces if desired.

Enjoy:

- Serve the Guacamole with Jicama Sticks and enjoy this tasty and healthy snack!

This combination is not only flavorful but also provides a satisfying crunch from the jicama. The creamy guacamole pairs perfectly with the crisp and slightly sweet jicama sticks. It's a great appetizer or snack for parties, gatherings, or a refreshing treat on a warm day. Adjust the ingredients to suit your taste preferences.

Spicy Roasted Chickpeas Recipe

Ingredients:

- 2 cans (15 oz each) chickpeas (garbanzo beans), drained and rinsed
- 2 tablespoons olive oil
- 1 teaspoon ground cumin
- 1 teaspoon smoked paprika
- 1/2 teaspoon cayenne pepper (adjust to taste for spiciness)
- 1/2 teaspoon garlic powder
- 1/2 teaspoon onion powder
- 1/2 teaspoon salt (adjust to taste)
- Freshly ground black pepper to taste

Instructions:

Preheat Oven:

- Preheat your oven to 400°F (200°C).

Dry Chickpeas:

- After draining and rinsing the chickpeas, pat them dry with a clean kitchen towel or paper towels. The drier they are, the crispier they will become.

Season Chickpeas:

- In a bowl, toss the chickpeas with olive oil, ground cumin, smoked paprika, cayenne pepper, garlic powder, onion powder, salt, and freshly ground black pepper. Ensure the chickpeas are well coated with the spice mixture.

Spread on Baking Sheet:

- Spread the seasoned chickpeas in a single layer on a baking sheet lined with parchment paper or a silicone baking mat.

Roast Chickpeas:

- Roast in the preheated oven for 25-35 minutes, or until the chickpeas are golden brown and crispy. Shake the pan or stir the chickpeas halfway through the cooking time to ensure even roasting.

Cool:

- Allow the roasted chickpeas to cool on the baking sheet. They will continue to crisp up as they cool.

Serve:

- Once cooled, transfer the spicy roasted chickpeas to a serving bowl.

Enjoy:

- Enjoy these Spicy Roasted Chickpeas as a crunchy and flavorful snack!

These chickpeas are not only delicious but also packed with protein and fiber. Adjust the level of spiciness to your liking, and feel free to experiment with additional seasonings such as chili powder, curry powder, or your favorite herbs. They make a great snack on their own or can be added to salads for an extra crunch.

Cucumber and Cream Cheese Roll-Ups Recipe

Ingredients:

- 1 large cucumber, washed and thinly sliced lengthwise
- 8 ounces cream cheese, softened
- 2 tablespoons fresh dill, chopped
- 1 tablespoon fresh chives, chopped
- Salt and black pepper to taste
- Optional: Smoked salmon slices for garnish

Instructions:

Prepare Cucumber Slices:

- Wash the cucumber and slice it thinly lengthwise using a mandoline or a vegetable peeler. Alternatively, you can use a knife for thin, even slices.

Prepare Cream Cheese Filling:

- In a bowl, combine softened cream cheese, chopped fresh dill, chopped chives, salt, and black pepper. Mix until well combined.

Spread Cream Cheese Mixture:

- Lay out the cucumber slices on a clean surface. Spread a thin layer of the cream cheese mixture over each cucumber slice.

Roll Up:

- If you're adding smoked salmon, place a small slice at the end of each cucumber slice. Roll up the cucumber slice, starting from the end with the cream cheese mixture, to create a roll-up.

Secure with Toothpick (Optional):

- If needed, secure each roll-up with a toothpick to keep it in place.

Chill (Optional):

- For a chilled appetizer, place the roll-ups in the refrigerator for about 15-20 minutes before serving.

Slice (Optional):

- If desired, slice the roll-ups into bite-sized pieces for a more elegant presentation.

Serve:

- Arrange the cucumber and cream cheese roll-ups on a serving platter.

Garnish (Optional):

- Garnish with additional fresh dill or chives.

Enjoy:

- Enjoy these light and flavorful Cucumber and Cream Cheese Roll-Ups as a delightful appetizer!

These roll-ups are not only tasty but also low-carb and gluten-free, making them a great option for various dietary preferences. You can get creative by adding other ingredients like smoked salmon, thinly sliced ham, or even roasted red pepper strips for extra flavor and color. They are perfect for parties, gatherings, or as a light and refreshing snack.

Avocado Salsa Recipe

Ingredients:

- 2 ripe avocados, diced
- 1 cup cherry tomatoes, halved
- 1/2 red onion, finely chopped
- 1 jalapeño, seeded and finely chopped (adjust to taste)
- 1/4 cup fresh cilantro, chopped
- Juice of 1 lime
- Salt and black pepper to taste

Instructions:

Prepare Avocados:

- Cut the avocados in half, remove the pit, and carefully dice the avocado flesh. Scoop the diced avocado into a mixing bowl.

Combine Ingredients:

- Add halved cherry tomatoes, finely chopped red onion, chopped jalapeño, and chopped fresh cilantro to the bowl with the diced avocados.

Add Lime Juice:

- Squeeze the juice of one lime over the ingredients in the bowl. The lime juice not only adds flavor but also helps prevent the avocados from browning.

Season:

- Season the avocado salsa with salt and black pepper to taste. Mix gently to combine all the ingredients.

Adjust Seasoning:

- Taste the salsa and adjust the seasoning, lime juice, or spiciness according to your preferences.

Chill (Optional):

- For enhanced flavors, you can refrigerate the avocado salsa for about 15-30 minutes before serving.

Serve:

- Spoon the avocado salsa into a serving bowl.

Garnish (Optional):

- Garnish with additional cilantro or a few lime wedges.

Enjoy:

- Serve the Avocado Salsa with tortilla chips, tacos, grilled meats, or as a topping for various dishes.

This Avocado Salsa is not only delicious but also adds a fresh and creamy element to your meals. Feel free to customize it by adding ingredients like diced mango, black beans, or corn for extra sweetness and texture. It's perfect for summer gatherings, picnics, or whenever you're craving a tasty and healthy topping.

Pistachio Trail Mix Recipe

Ingredients:

- 1 cup shelled pistachios
- 1 cup almonds, whole or sliced
- 1/2 cup dried cranberries
- 1/2 cup golden raisins
- 1/2 cup dark chocolate chips or chunks
- 1/4 cup pumpkin seeds (pepitas)
- 1/4 teaspoon sea salt (optional)

Instructions:

Prepare Pistachios:

- If the pistachios are not already shelled, remove the shells to get 1 cup of shelled pistachios.

Combine Ingredients:

- In a large bowl, combine the shelled pistachios, almonds, dried cranberries, golden raisins, dark chocolate chips or chunks, and pumpkin seeds.

Mix Well:

- Gently mix the ingredients until they are evenly distributed.

Add Salt (Optional):

- If you like a hint of saltiness, sprinkle sea salt over the trail mix and toss to combine. Adjust the amount of salt to your taste.

Store:

- Transfer the pistachio trail mix to an airtight container or portion it into small snack bags for on-the-go convenience.

Enjoy:

- Enjoy the Pistachio Trail Mix as a delicious and energy-boosting snack!

This trail mix is not only tasty but also provides a mix of healthy fats, protein, and natural sweetness. Pistachios add a unique flavor and texture, and the combination of nuts, dried fruits, and chocolate creates a well-balanced snack. Feel free to customize the trail mix by adding your favorite nuts, seeds, or dried fruits. It's perfect for hikes, road trips, or a quick and nutritious snack at any time.

Cottage Cheese Stuffed Bell Peppers Recipe

Ingredients:

- 4 large bell peppers (any color)
- 2 cups cottage cheese
- 1 cup cooked quinoa or rice
- 1 cup cherry tomatoes, diced
- 1/2 cup red onion, finely chopped
- 1/2 cup fresh parsley, chopped
- 1/2 cup feta cheese, crumbled (optional)
- 2 cloves garlic, minced
- 1 teaspoon dried oregano
- Salt and black pepper to taste
- Olive oil for drizzling
- Grated Parmesan cheese for topping (optional)

Instructions:

Preheat Oven:

- Preheat your oven to 375°F (190°C).

Prepare Bell Peppers:

- Cut the tops off the bell peppers, remove the seeds and membranes. If needed, trim the bottoms slightly to help them stand upright.

Prepare Filling:

- In a large bowl, combine cottage cheese, cooked quinoa or rice, diced cherry tomatoes, chopped red onion, fresh parsley, crumbled feta cheese (if using), minced garlic, dried oregano, salt, and black pepper. Mix well to combine.

Stuff Peppers:
- Stuff each bell pepper with the cottage cheese mixture, pressing down gently to pack the filling.

Drizzle with Olive Oil:
- Drizzle a little olive oil over the top of each stuffed bell pepper.

Bake:
- Place the stuffed bell peppers in a baking dish. Bake in the preheated oven for 25-30 minutes or until the peppers are tender.

Optional Parmesan Topping:
- If desired, sprinkle grated Parmesan cheese over the stuffed peppers during the last 10 minutes of baking.

Check Doneness:
- Check the doneness by inserting a fork into the peppers; it should go in easily when they are done.

Serve:
- Remove from the oven and let them cool slightly before serving.

Enjoy:
- Enjoy these Cottage Cheese Stuffed Bell Peppers as a wholesome and flavorful meal!

This recipe provides a balanced mix of protein from cottage cheese and quinoa or rice, along with the freshness of vegetables and herbs. Feel free to customize the filling with your favorite ingredients, such as spinach, black beans, or different types of cheese. It's a delicious and nutritious dish that can be served as a main course or a satisfying side dish.

Crispy Kale Chips Recipe

Ingredients:

- 1 bunch of kale (about 8 cups, stems removed and torn into bite-sized pieces)
- 1-2 tablespoons olive oil
- 1/2 teaspoon salt (adjust to taste)
- Optional seasonings: garlic powder, onion powder, paprika, nutritional yeast, or cayenne pepper for added flavor

Instructions:

Preheat Oven:

- Preheat your oven to 300°F (150°C).

Prepare Kale:

- Wash the kale leaves thoroughly and ensure they are completely dry. Remove the tough stems and tear the leaves into bite-sized pieces.

Massage with Olive Oil:

- In a large bowl, toss the kale pieces with olive oil. Massage the oil into the leaves to ensure each piece is lightly coated.

Season:

- Sprinkle salt over the kale and add any optional seasonings you prefer. Toss again to distribute the seasonings evenly.

Arrange on Baking Sheet:

- Arrange the kale pieces in a single layer on a baking sheet. Avoid overcrowding to ensure even crisping.

Bake:

- Bake in the preheated oven for 10-15 minutes, or until the edges of the kale are crispy and they have a nice, deep green color. Keep an eye on them to prevent burning.

Cool:

- Allow the kale chips to cool on the baking sheet for a few minutes. They will continue to crisp up as they cool.

Serve:

- Serve the crispy kale chips immediately as a healthy and crunchy snack.

Enjoy:

- Enjoy these nutritious and flavorful kale chips on their own or as a topping for salads and soups!

Kale chips are a great alternative to traditional potato chips, offering a satisfying crunch along with plenty of nutrients. Experiment with different seasonings to find your favorite flavor combination. Store any leftovers in an airtight container to maintain their crispiness. They make for a perfect guilt-free snack!

Edamame Hummus Recipe

Ingredients:

- 1 1/2 cups frozen edamame, shelled
- 1/4 cup tahini
- 1/4 cup extra-virgin olive oil
- 2 cloves garlic, minced
- Juice of 1 lemon
- 1/2 teaspoon ground cumin
- Salt and black pepper to taste
- Water (as needed for desired consistency)
- Optional: Paprika, sesame seeds, or chopped fresh parsley for garnish

Instructions:

Cook Edamame:

- Cook the shelled edamame according to the package instructions. Usually, they are blanched in boiling water for about 3-5 minutes. Drain and set aside.

Prepare Edamame Hummus:

- In a food processor, combine the cooked edamame, tahini, extra-virgin olive oil, minced garlic, lemon juice, ground cumin, salt, and black pepper.

Blend:

- Blend the ingredients until smooth, stopping to scrape down the sides of the food processor as needed.

Adjust Consistency:

- If the hummus is too thick, you can add water, one tablespoon at a time, until you reach your desired consistency.

Taste and Adjust:

- Taste the edamame hummus and adjust the seasoning, adding more salt, pepper, or lemon juice if necessary.

Serve:

- Transfer the edamame hummus to a serving bowl.

Garnish (Optional):

- Drizzle with extra-virgin olive oil, and sprinkle with paprika, sesame seeds, or chopped fresh parsley for garnish.

Enjoy:

- Enjoy the Edamame Hummus with pita bread, vegetable sticks, or as a spread on sandwiches!

This edamame hummus is not only delicious but also packed with protein and fiber. It makes a fantastic and nutritious dip or spread. Feel free to customize the recipe by adding a touch of your favorite herbs or spices. It's a great way to introduce a unique and vibrant twist to your hummus!

Cream Cheese Stuffed Bell Peppers Recipe

Ingredients:

- 4 large bell peppers (any color)
- 8 oz cream cheese, softened
- 1 cup cooked quinoa or rice
- 1 cup black beans, drained and rinsed
- 1 cup corn kernels (fresh, frozen, or canned)
- 1 cup diced tomatoes
- 1/2 cup red onion, finely chopped
- 1/2 cup shredded cheddar or Mexican blend cheese
- 2 cloves garlic, minced
- 1 teaspoon ground cumin
- 1 teaspoon chili powder
- Salt and black pepper to taste
- Fresh cilantro or green onions for garnish (optional)

Instructions:

Preheat Oven:

- Preheat your oven to 375°F (190°C).

Prepare Bell Peppers:

- Cut the tops off the bell peppers, remove the seeds and membranes. If needed, trim the bottoms slightly to help them stand upright.

Prepare Filling:

- In a large bowl, mix together softened cream cheese, cooked quinoa or rice, black beans, corn kernels, diced tomatoes, red onion, shredded cheese, minced garlic, ground cumin, chili powder, salt, and black pepper.

Stuff Peppers:
- Spoon the cream cheese filling into each bell pepper, pressing down gently to pack the filling.

Bake:
- Place the stuffed bell peppers in a baking dish. Bake in the preheated oven for 25-30 minutes or until the peppers are tender.

Optional Cheese Topping:
- If desired, sprinkle additional cheese on top of each stuffed pepper during the last 10 minutes of baking.

Check Doneness:
- Check the doneness by inserting a fork into the peppers; it should go in easily when they are done.

Garnish:
- Garnish with fresh cilantro or green onions if desired.

Serve:
- Remove from the oven and let them cool slightly before serving.

Enjoy:
- Enjoy these Cream Cheese Stuffed Bell Peppers as a flavorful and satisfying meal!

This recipe combines the creamy texture of cream cheese with the wholesome goodness of quinoa, black beans, and vegetables. It's a delicious and comforting dish that can be customized with your favorite spices and herbs. Serve them as a main course or a tasty side dish for a wholesome and satisfying meal.

Greek Yogurt Bark Recipe

Ingredients:

- 2 cups Greek yogurt (full-fat or low-fat)
- 2-3 tablespoons honey or maple syrup (adjust to taste)
- 1 teaspoon vanilla extract
- Toppings: Fresh berries, sliced fruits, nuts, seeds, granola, or shredded coconut

Instructions:

Prepare Greek Yogurt Mixture:

- In a bowl, combine Greek yogurt, honey or maple syrup, and vanilla extract. Mix well until smooth and well combined.

Line a Baking Sheet:

- Line a baking sheet with parchment paper or a silicone baking mat.

Spread Yogurt Mixture:

- Pour the Greek yogurt mixture onto the prepared baking sheet and spread it evenly into a thin layer using a spatula.

Add Toppings:

- Sprinkle your choice of toppings evenly over the Greek yogurt layer. You can use fresh berries, sliced fruits, nuts, seeds, granola, shredded coconut, or a combination of these.

Freeze:

- Place the baking sheet in the freezer and let the Greek yogurt bark freeze for at least 3-4 hours or until completely solid.

Break into Pieces:

- Once frozen, remove the bark from the freezer. Use a knife to break it into bite-sized pieces or irregular shards.

Serve:
- Serve the Greek Yogurt Bark immediately as a refreshing and nutritious frozen treat.

Store:
- If you have any leftovers, store them in an airtight container in the freezer for later enjoyment.

Enjoy:
- Enjoy this guilt-free and delicious Greek Yogurt Bark!

Feel free to get creative with your toppings and experiment with different combinations. This recipe is versatile, and you can tailor it to your taste preferences or dietary needs. It's a perfect snack or dessert, especially during warmer months.

Cheese and Nut Platter Recipe

Cheese Selection:

Brie: A soft and creamy cheese with a mild flavor.
Cheddar: A sharp and aged cheese that adds richness.
Gouda: A semi-hard cheese with a nutty flavor.
Blue Cheese: For a bold and tangy element.
Goat Cheese (Chevre): Creamy and slightly tangy.

Nut Selection:

Almonds: Roasted or smoked almonds add crunch.
Walnuts: Provide a rich, earthy flavor.
Pecans: Sweet and buttery, complementing various cheeses.
Cashews: Mild and creamy.
Pistachios: A colorful and flavorful addition.

Accompaniments:

Fresh Fruits: Grapes, apple slices, and figs add sweetness.
Dried Fruits: Apricots, dates, or figs provide a chewy texture.
Crackers and Bread: A variety of crackers, breadsticks, and sliced baguette.
Honey: Drizzle honey for a touch of sweetness.
Jams or Preserves: Fig or apricot preserves pair well with cheeses.
Mustard: Whole grain or Dijon mustard complements the flavors.
Olives: Green or black olives for a briny element.
Pickles: Cornichons or pickled onions for acidity.

Assembly:

Cheese Placement:
- Arrange the cheeses on a large serving platter, leaving space between each type.

Nut Distribution:
- Scatter the assorted nuts evenly around the cheeses.

Fruit Arrangement:
- Place fresh and dried fruits in clusters, spreading them throughout the platter.

Cracker and Bread Placement:
- Artfully arrange a variety of crackers and bread around the cheeses.

Condiment Presentation:
- Add small bowls or jars for honey, jams, mustard, and olives. Place them strategically on the platter.

Garnish (Optional):
- Garnish with fresh herbs, such as rosemary or thyme, for a decorative touch.

Serve:
- Serve the cheese and nut platter with small cheese knives, allowing guests to sample various combinations.

Wine Pairing (Optional):
- Consider pairing the platter with a selection of wines that complement the cheeses.

Enjoy:
- Invite guests to mix and match the cheeses, nuts, and accompaniments for a delightful tasting experience.

Remember to consider dietary preferences and restrictions when choosing cheeses and accompaniments. This Cheese and Nut Platter is versatile and can be adapted to suit different occasions and preferences.

Roasted Chickpeas Recipe

Ingredients:

- 2 cans (15 oz each) chickpeas (garbanzo beans), drained and rinsed
- 2 tablespoons olive oil
- 1 teaspoon ground cumin
- 1 teaspoon smoked paprika
- 1/2 teaspoon garlic powder
- 1/2 teaspoon onion powder
- 1/2 teaspoon chili powder (adjust to taste)
- Salt and black pepper to taste

Instructions:

Preheat Oven:

- Preheat your oven to 400°F (200°C).

Prepare Chickpeas:

- Drain and rinse the chickpeas. Pat them dry with a clean kitchen towel or paper towels. Remove any loose skins.

Season Chickpeas:

- In a bowl, toss the chickpeas with olive oil, ground cumin, smoked paprika, garlic powder, onion powder, chili powder, salt, and black pepper. Ensure the chickpeas are well coated with the spice mixture.

Spread on Baking Sheet:

- Spread the seasoned chickpeas in a single layer on a baking sheet lined with parchment paper or a silicone baking mat.

Roast Chickpeas:

- Roast in the preheated oven for 25-35 minutes, or until the chickpeas are golden brown and crispy. Shake the pan or stir the chickpeas halfway through the cooking time to ensure even roasting.

Cool:
- Allow the roasted chickpeas to cool on the baking sheet. They will continue to crisp up as they cool.

Serve:
- Once cooled, transfer the roasted chickpeas to a serving bowl.

Enjoy:
- Enjoy these Spicy Roasted Chickpeas as a crunchy and flavorful snack!

Feel free to adjust the seasonings to your taste preferences. Roasted chickpeas can be stored in an airtight container at room temperature for a few days, but keep in mind that they are crispiest when freshly made. They make for a great snack on their own, or you can add them to salads or trail mix for an extra crunch.

Tzatziki Sauce Recipe

Ingredients:

- 1 cup Greek yogurt
- 1/2 cucumber, peeled, seeded, and finely diced
- 2 cloves garlic, minced
- 1 tablespoon fresh dill, chopped
- 1 tablespoon fresh mint, chopped
- 1 tablespoon extra-virgin olive oil
- 1 teaspoon lemon juice
- Salt and black pepper to taste

Instructions:

Prepare Cucumber:

- Peel, seed, and finely dice half of a cucumber.

Prepare Tzatziki Sauce:

- In a bowl, combine Greek yogurt, diced cucumber, minced garlic, chopped fresh dill, chopped fresh mint, extra-virgin olive oil, lemon juice, salt, and black pepper.

Mix Well:

- Mix the ingredients until well combined. Adjust salt and pepper according to your taste.

Chill (Optional):

- For enhanced flavors, you can refrigerate the tzatziki sauce for about 30 minutes before serving.

Cucumber Slices with Tzatziki

Ingredients:

- 2 large cucumbers, washed and sliced into rounds
- Tzatziki sauce (prepared from the above recipe)

Instructions:

Slice Cucumbers:

- Wash the cucumbers and slice them into rounds.

Arrange on a Plate:

- Arrange the cucumber slices on a serving plate.

Top with Tzatziki:

- Spoon a dollop of tzatziki sauce onto each cucumber slice.

Garnish (Optional):

- Garnish with additional chopped fresh herbs or a drizzle of olive oil if desired.

Serve:

- Serve the Cucumber Slices with Tzatziki immediately and enjoy this light and refreshing snack!

This dish is not only delicious but also a healthy and low-calorie option. The crispness of the cucumber pairs perfectly with the creamy and flavorful tzatziki sauce. It's a great option for summer gatherings, parties, or a quick and satisfying snack.

Deviled Eggs Recipe

Ingredients:

- 6 large eggs
- 2 tablespoons mayonnaise
- 1 teaspoon Dijon mustard
- 1 teaspoon white vinegar
- 1/2 teaspoon salt
- 1/4 teaspoon black pepper
- Paprika and fresh chives for garnish

Instructions:

Boil the Eggs:

- Place the eggs in a single layer in a saucepan and cover with water. Bring the water to a boil, then reduce the heat to low and simmer for 10 minutes. Remove from heat and place the eggs in cold water to cool.

Peel the Eggs:

- Once the eggs are cool, peel them and cut them in half lengthwise.

Remove Yolks:

- Carefully remove the yolks from the egg halves and place them in a bowl. Set aside the egg whites.

Prepare Filling:

- Mash the egg yolks with a fork. Add mayonnaise, Dijon mustard, white vinegar, salt, and black pepper. Mix until smooth and well combined.

Fill the Egg Whites:

- Spoon or pipe the yolk mixture back into the egg white halves.

Garnish:

- Sprinkle with paprika and garnish with fresh chives.

Chill (Optional):

- For enhanced flavors, you can chill the deviled eggs in the refrigerator for about 30 minutes before serving.

Serve:

- Arrange the Deviled Eggs on a serving platter and enjoy!

Deviled eggs are a versatile dish, and you can customize the filling to suit your taste. Feel free to experiment with additional ingredients like finely chopped herbs, pickle relish, or a dash of hot sauce for some extra kick. They make a fantastic appetizer for gatherings, brunches, or as a simple and satisfying snack.

Desserts

Sugar-Free Apple Crisp Recipe

Ingredients:

For the Apple Filling:

- 6 cups peeled, cored, and sliced apples (a mix of sweet and tart varieties)
- 1 tablespoon lemon juice
- 1 teaspoon ground cinnamon
- 1/2 teaspoon ground nutmeg
- 1/4 cup sugar substitute (like erythritol or stevia)

For the Crisp Topping:

- 1 cup old-fashioned oats
- 1/2 cup almond flour
- 1/4 cup chopped nuts (such as pecans or walnuts)
- 1/4 cup melted coconut oil or butter
- 1 teaspoon ground cinnamon
- 1/4 cup sugar substitute
- A pinch of salt

Instructions:

Preheat Oven:

- Preheat your oven to 350°F (175°C).

Prepare the Apple Filling:

- In a large bowl, toss the sliced apples with lemon juice, ground cinnamon, ground nutmeg, and sugar substitute. Transfer the seasoned apples to a baking dish.

Prepare the Crisp Topping:

- In another bowl, combine oats, almond flour, chopped nuts, melted coconut oil or butter, ground cinnamon, sugar substitute, and a pinch of salt. Mix until everything is well combined.

Assemble the Crisp:

- Evenly spread the crisp topping over the apple mixture in the baking dish.

Bake:

- Bake in the preheated oven for about 35-40 minutes or until the top is golden brown, and the apples are tender.

Cool:

- Allow the sugar-free apple crisp to cool for a few minutes before serving.

Serve:

- Serve warm, and optionally, top with a dollop of sugar-free whipped cream or a scoop of sugar-free vanilla ice cream.

Enjoy:

- Enjoy this delicious and guilt-free Sugar-Free Apple Crisp!

Feel free to adjust the sweetness level according to your taste preferences. This recipe allows you to enjoy the comforting flavors of apple crisp without added sugars. It's a perfect dessert for those looking for a healthier, low-sugar alternative.

Almond Butter Cookies Recipe

Ingredients:

- 1 cup almond butter (unsweetened and creamy)
- 1/2 cup sugar substitute (e.g., erythritol, stevia, or monk fruit)
- 1 large egg
- 1 teaspoon vanilla extract
- 1/2 teaspoon baking soda
- 1/4 teaspoon salt
- Optional: Dark chocolate chips or chopped almonds for added texture

Instructions:

Preheat Oven:

- Preheat your oven to 350°F (175°C). Line a baking sheet with parchment paper.

Combine Wet Ingredients:

- In a bowl, combine almond butter, sugar substitute, egg, and vanilla extract. Mix until well combined.

Add Dry Ingredients:

- Add baking soda and salt to the wet ingredients. Mix until the dough comes together.

Optional Add-Ins:

- If desired, fold in dark chocolate chips or chopped almonds to add texture and flavor to the cookies.

Shape Cookies:

- Scoop tablespoon-sized portions of dough and roll them into balls. Place them on the prepared baking sheet, leaving space between each cookie.

Flatten Cookies (Optional):

- Use a fork to flatten each cookie slightly, creating a crisscross pattern on top.

Bake:

- Bake in the preheated oven for 10-12 minutes or until the edges are lightly golden.

Cool:

- Allow the cookies to cool on the baking sheet for a few minutes before transferring them to a wire rack to cool completely.

Serve:

- Serve and enjoy these delicious almond butter cookies!

These almond butter cookies are gluten-free and lower in carbs compared to traditional cookies. The almond butter provides a rich and nutty flavor, and you can customize the recipe by adding your favorite mix-ins. They are a great option for those looking for a healthier cookie alternative.

Sugar-Free Lemon Sorbet Recipe

Ingredients:

- 1 cup freshly squeezed lemon juice (about 5-6 lemons)
- 1 cup water
- 1/2 cup sugar substitute (e.g., erythritol, stevia, or monk fruit)
- Zest of 1 lemon
- 1 teaspoon lemon extract (optional, for extra flavor)

Instructions:

Prepare Lemon Juice:

- Squeeze lemons to obtain 1 cup of fresh lemon juice. Strain to remove seeds and pulp if desired.

Make Simple Syrup:

- In a small saucepan, combine water and sugar substitute over medium heat. Stir until the sugar substitute is completely dissolved, and the mixture forms a simple syrup. Allow it to cool.

Combine Ingredients:

- In a mixing bowl, combine the fresh lemon juice, lemon zest, and the cooled sugar substitute simple syrup. If you'd like a more intense lemon flavor, add the optional lemon extract.

Chill Mixture:

- Place the mixture in the refrigerator to chill for at least 1-2 hours.

Freeze:

- Pour the chilled lemon mixture into an ice cream maker and churn according to the manufacturer's instructions until it reaches a sorbet consistency.

Transfer to Container:

- Transfer the sorbet to a lidded container and freeze for an additional 3-4 hours or until firm.

Serve:

- Scoop the sugar-free lemon sorbet into bowls or cones, and enjoy this refreshing and tangy treat!

Garnish (Optional):

- Garnish with a lemon twist or mint leaves for an extra touch of freshness.

This sugar-free lemon sorbet is not only a delightful dessert but also a cool and refreshing palate cleanser. Adjust the level of sweetness according to your taste preferences. It's perfect for hot summer days or as a light and zesty ending to a meal.

Pumpkin Pie Chia Pudding Recipe

Ingredients:

For the Pumpkin Layer:

- 1/2 cup canned pumpkin puree
- 1/2 cup unsweetened almond milk (or any milk of your choice)
- 2 tablespoons chia seeds
- 1-2 tablespoons maple syrup or sweetener of your choice
- 1/2 teaspoon pumpkin pie spice (or a mix of cinnamon, nutmeg, and cloves)
- 1/2 teaspoon vanilla extract

For the Vanilla Chia Layer:

- 1/4 cup chia seeds
- 1 cup unsweetened almond milk (or any milk of your choice)
- 1-2 tablespoons maple syrup or sweetener of your choice
- 1/2 teaspoon vanilla extract

Instructions:

Prepare Pumpkin Layer:

- In a bowl, whisk together the pumpkin puree, almond milk, chia seeds, maple syrup, pumpkin pie spice, and vanilla extract. Make sure the ingredients are well combined. Let it sit for a few minutes to allow the chia seeds to absorb the liquid.

Prepare Vanilla Chia Layer:

- In another bowl, whisk together the chia seeds, almond milk, maple syrup, and vanilla extract. Let it sit for a few minutes as well.

Layering:

- In serving glasses or jars, layer the pumpkin chia mixture and the vanilla chia mixture alternately.

Chill:

- Cover the glasses or jars and refrigerate for at least 2-3 hours or overnight to allow the chia pudding to set.

Serve:

- Once set, give the pudding a good stir to evenly distribute the layers. You can top it with a dollop of whipped cream or a sprinkle of pumpkin pie spice if desired.

Enjoy:

- Enjoy this delicious Pumpkin Pie Chia Pudding as a wholesome dessert or a nutritious breakfast!

This recipe combines the creamy texture of chia pudding with the warm and comforting flavors of pumpkin pie. It's a great way to indulge in the taste of fall while still maintaining a healthy and satisfying treat.

Raspberry Coconut Panna Cotta Recipe

Ingredients:

For the Coconut Panna Cotta:

- 1 can (13.5 oz) coconut milk (full-fat)
- 1/2 cup sugar or sweetener of your choice
- 1 teaspoon vanilla extract
- 2 teaspoons unflavored gelatin
- 2 tablespoons cold water

For the Raspberry Coulis:

- 1 cup fresh or frozen raspberries
- 2 tablespoons sugar or sweetener of your choice
- 1 tablespoon lemon juice

For Garnish:

- Fresh raspberries
- Shredded coconut

Instructions:

1. Prepare Coconut Panna Cotta:

   In a small bowl, sprinkle gelatin over cold water. Let it sit for a few minutes to bloom.

   In a saucepan, heat the coconut milk and sugar over medium heat, stirring until the sugar dissolves. Do not bring it to a boil.

Remove the coconut milk mixture from heat, add the bloomed gelatin, and stir until the gelatin is completely dissolved.

Stir in the vanilla extract.

Pour the coconut panna cotta mixture into serving glasses or molds. Refrigerate for at least 4 hours or until set.

2. Prepare Raspberry Coulis:

In a small saucepan, combine raspberries, sugar, and lemon juice.

Heat over medium heat, stirring occasionally, until the raspberries break down and the mixture thickens.

Remove from heat and strain the coulis through a fine-mesh sieve to remove seeds. Allow it to cool.

3. Assemble:

Once the coconut panna cotta is set, spoon a layer of raspberry coulis over the top.

Garnish with fresh raspberries and shredded coconut.

4. Serve:

Serve chilled and enjoy this Raspberry Coconut Panna Cotta as a luxurious and flavorful dessert!

This dessert is not only visually appealing but also offers a delightful combination of creamy coconut and tart raspberry flavors. It's perfect for special occasions or when you want to treat yourself to something indulgent.

Walnut and Date Energy Balls Recipe

Ingredients:

- 1 cup pitted dates
- 1 cup walnuts
- 1/4 cup unsweetened shredded coconut
- 1 tablespoon chia seeds (optional)
- 1 tablespoon flaxseeds (optional)
- 1 teaspoon vanilla extract
- A pinch of salt

Optional Coatings:

- Additional shredded coconut
- Finely chopped walnuts

Instructions:

Prepare Dates:

- If the dates are not already soft, soak them in warm water for 10-15 minutes to soften. Drain well.

Blend Walnuts:

- In a food processor, blend walnuts until they are finely chopped.

Add Dates and Other Ingredients:

- Add the pitted dates, shredded coconut, chia seeds, flaxseeds, vanilla extract, and a pinch of salt to the food processor with the chopped walnuts.

Blend Until Combined:

- Process the mixture until it forms a sticky and uniform dough. If the mixture seems too dry, you can add a few more dates or a teaspoon of water.

Form Energy Balls:

- Scoop out small portions of the mixture and roll them between your palms to form bite-sized energy balls.

Optional Coatings:

- Roll the energy balls in additional shredded coconut or finely chopped walnuts for a coating.

Chill:

- Place the energy balls in the refrigerator for at least 30 minutes to firm up.

Store:

- Store the Walnut and Date Energy Balls in an airtight container in the refrigerator. They can also be stored in the freezer for longer shelf life.

Enjoy:

- Grab these energy balls as a quick snack for a burst of natural energy!

These Walnut and Date Energy Balls are not only delicious but also packed with nutrients from the dates and walnuts. They make for a convenient and healthy snack that you can enjoy on the go. Feel free to customize the recipe by adding other ingredients like cocoa powder, cinnamon, or nut butter for extra flavor.

Dark Chocolate Covered Strawberries Recipe

Ingredients:

- Fresh strawberries, washed and dried
- Dark chocolate chips or chopped dark chocolate (70% cocoa or higher)
- White chocolate chips (optional, for drizzling)
- Toppings (optional): Chopped nuts, shredded coconut, sprinkles

Instructions:

Prepare Strawberries:

- Wash and thoroughly dry the strawberries. It's crucial to have dry strawberries to help the chocolate adhere.

Melt Dark Chocolate:

- In a heatproof bowl, melt the dark chocolate in the microwave using 30-second intervals, stirring after each interval until smooth. Alternatively, you can melt the chocolate using a double boiler.

Dip Strawberries:

- Hold each strawberry by the stem and dip it into the melted dark chocolate, covering it about two-thirds of the way. Allow any excess chocolate to drip back into the bowl.

Place on Parchment Paper:

- Place the chocolate-covered strawberries on a parchment paper-lined tray or plate. Make sure they are not touching each other.

Optional Toppings:

- If desired, sprinkle or roll the dipped strawberries in toppings like chopped nuts, shredded coconut, or sprinkles while the chocolate is still wet.

Melt White Chocolate (Optional):

- If you want to drizzle white chocolate over the dark chocolate-covered strawberries, melt the white chocolate in a separate bowl using the same method as for the dark chocolate.

Drizzle White Chocolate (Optional):

- Using a fork or a piping bag, drizzle the melted white chocolate over the dark chocolate-covered strawberries. This adds a decorative touch.

Chill:

- Place the tray of chocolate-covered strawberries in the refrigerator for about 30 minutes or until the chocolate is fully set.

Serve:

- Once the chocolate is set, remove the strawberries from the refrigerator. Arrange them on a serving plate and enjoy!

Dark Chocolate Covered Strawberries are perfect for special occasions, romantic evenings, or as an elegant dessert. They also make a lovely gift. Be creative with toppings and decorations to make them even more special.

Chocolate Avocado Mousse Recipe

Ingredients:

- 2 ripe avocados, peeled and pitted
- 1/4 cup unsweetened cocoa powder
- 1/4 cup maple syrup or agave nectar (adjust to taste)
- 1/4 cup almond milk or any milk of your choice
- 1 teaspoon vanilla extract
- A pinch of salt
- Optional toppings: Fresh berries, chopped nuts, shredded coconut

Instructions:

Blend Avocado:

- In a food processor or blender, combine the ripe avocados, cocoa powder, maple syrup, almond milk, vanilla extract, and a pinch of salt.

Blend Until Smooth:

- Blend the ingredients until smooth and creamy. Stop and scrape down the sides as needed.

Adjust Sweetness:

- Taste the mousse and adjust the sweetness if necessary by adding more maple syrup or sweetener of your choice.

Chill (Optional):

- For a firmer texture, you can refrigerate the chocolate avocado mousse for 1-2 hours.

Serve:

- Spoon the chocolate avocado mousse into serving bowls or glasses.

Optional Toppings:

- Top with fresh berries, chopped nuts, or shredded coconut for added texture and flavor.

Enjoy:

- Serve and enjoy this luscious and guilt-free Chocolate Avocado Mousse!

This dessert is not only delicious but also packed with healthy fats from avocados. It's a great option for those looking for a dairy-free and lower-sugar alternative to traditional chocolate mousse. The creamy texture of avocados makes this mousse incredibly smooth and satisfying.

Chocolate Avocado Mousse Recipe

Ingredients:

- 2 ripe avocados, peeled and pitted
- 1/4 cup cocoa powder (unsweetened)
- 1/4 cup maple syrup or honey (adjust to taste)
- 1 teaspoon vanilla extract
- Pinch of salt
- Optional toppings: Fresh berries, shaved chocolate, whipped cream

Instructions:

Blend Ingredients:

- In a food processor or blender, combine the ripe avocados, cocoa powder, maple syrup or honey, vanilla extract, and a pinch of salt.

Blend Until Smooth:

- Blend the ingredients until smooth and creamy. You may need to stop and scrape down the sides of the blender or food processor a few times to ensure everything is well incorporated.

Adjust Sweetness:

- Taste the mousse and adjust the sweetness by adding more maple syrup or honey if desired.

Chill:

- Transfer the chocolate avocado mousse to serving bowls or glasses. Cover and refrigerate for at least 30 minutes to allow it to chill and set.

Serve:

- Once chilled, serve the chocolate avocado mousse with your choice of toppings, such as fresh berries, shaved chocolate, or a dollop of whipped cream.

Enjoy:

- Enjoy this creamy and indulgent Chocolate Avocado Mousse as a guilt-free dessert or snack!

This dessert is not only delicious but also packed with healthy fats and nutrients from the avocado. It's a great option for those looking for a healthier alternative to traditional mousse recipes. Plus, it's vegan and gluten-free, making it suitable for a variety of dietary preferences.

Coconut Flour Banana Bread Recipe

Ingredients:

- 4 ripe bananas, mashed
- 4 large eggs
- 1/2 cup coconut flour
- 1/4 cup melted coconut oil
- 1/4 cup honey or maple syrup
- 1 teaspoon vanilla extract
- 1 teaspoon baking soda
- 1/2 teaspoon ground cinnamon
- A pinch of salt
- Optional add-ins: Chopped nuts, chocolate chips, or shredded coconut

Instructions:

Preheat Oven:

- Preheat your oven to 350°F (175°C). Grease a standard-sized loaf pan or line it with parchment paper.

Mash Bananas:

- In a large bowl, mash the ripe bananas with a fork or potato masher.

Add Wet Ingredients:

- Add the eggs, melted coconut oil, honey or maple syrup, and vanilla extract to the mashed bananas. Mix well until the ingredients are combined.

Add Dry Ingredients:

- In the same bowl, add the coconut flour, baking soda, ground cinnamon, and a pinch of salt. Mix until the batter is smooth and well combined.

Optional Add-Ins:

- If desired, fold in chopped nuts, chocolate chips, or shredded coconut into the batter.

Pour into Pan:

- Pour the batter into the prepared loaf pan, spreading it evenly.

Bake:

- Bake in the preheated oven for 50-60 minutes or until a toothpick inserted into the center comes out clean.

Cool:

- Allow the coconut flour banana bread to cool in the pan for about 10 minutes, then transfer it to a wire rack to cool completely.

Slice and Serve:

- Once cooled, slice the banana bread and serve. Enjoy!

This Coconut Flour Banana Bread is moist, flavorful, and a great option for those following a gluten-free or grain-free diet. Feel free to customize it with your favorite add-ins and enjoy a healthy and delicious treat.

Sugar-Free Berry Sorbet Recipe

Ingredients:

- 3 cups mixed berries (such as strawberries, blueberries, raspberries)
- 1-2 tablespoons lemon juice (adjust to taste)
- 1-2 tablespoons sugar substitute (e.g., erythritol, stevia, or monk fruit)
- 1/2 cup water

Instructions:

Prepare Berries:

- Wash and hull the strawberries if using. Ensure all berries are clean.

Blend Berries:

- In a blender or food processor, combine the mixed berries, lemon juice, sugar substitute, and water.

Blend Until Smooth:

- Blend the mixture until smooth. If the sorbet is too thick, you can add a bit more water to achieve your desired consistency.

Taste and Adjust:

- Taste the sorbet and adjust the sweetness by adding more sugar substitute or lemon juice according to your preference.

Strain (Optional):

- If you prefer a smoother sorbet, you can strain the mixture using a fine-mesh sieve to remove seeds and pulp.

Chill:

- Transfer the sorbet mixture to a shallow dish and spread it evenly. Place it in the freezer.

Freeze:

- Freeze the sorbet for about 4 hours, or until it's firm around the edges.

Blend Again (Optional):

- Once the edges are firm, take the sorbet out of the freezer and blend it again to break any ice crystals. This step is optional but helps create a smoother texture.

Freeze Again:

- Return the sorbet to the freezer and freeze for an additional 2-3 hours or until it's completely set.

Serve:

- Scoop the sugar-free berry sorbet into bowls or cones and enjoy this delightful and healthy dessert!

This Sugar-Free Berry Sorbet is a perfect way to enjoy the natural sweetness of berries without the need for added sugars. It's a light and refreshing treat, making it ideal for hot days or as a guilt-free dessert option.

Almond Joy Energy Bites Recipe

Ingredients:

- 1 cup rolled oats
- 1/2 cup almond butter
- 1/4 cup honey or maple syrup
- 1/4 cup shredded coconut (unsweetened)
- 1/4 cup chopped almonds
- 1/4 cup dark chocolate chips
- 1 teaspoon vanilla extract
- A pinch of salt

Instructions:

Combine Ingredients:

- In a large bowl, combine rolled oats, almond butter, honey or maple syrup, shredded coconut, chopped almonds, dark chocolate chips, vanilla extract, and a pinch of salt.

Mix Well:

- Mix the ingredients thoroughly until the mixture is well combined.

Chill:

- Place the mixture in the refrigerator for about 30 minutes to make it easier to handle.

Form Bites:

- Once chilled, take small portions of the mixture and roll them between your palms to form bite-sized energy balls.

Optional Coating (If Desired):

- Roll the energy bites in additional shredded coconut or finely chopped almonds for a coating.

Chill Again (Optional):

- If the energy bites are too soft, you can place them in the refrigerator for an additional 30 minutes to firm up.

Store:

- Store the Almond Joy Energy Bites in an airtight container in the refrigerator for freshness.

Enjoy:

- Enjoy these tasty and wholesome energy bites as a quick and satisfying snack!

These Almond Joy Energy Bites are packed with oats, almond butter, nuts, and dark chocolate, providing a balance of energy and nutrients. They are perfect for a pre-workout snack or as a mid-afternoon pick-me-up. Feel free to customize the recipe by adding your favorite ingredients or adjusting sweetness to suit your taste.

Coconut Flour Pancakes Recipe

Ingredients:

- 1/4 cup coconut flour
- 1/2 teaspoon baking powder
- Pinch of salt
- 3 large eggs
- 1/4 cup coconut milk or almond milk
- 1 tablespoon melted coconut oil or butter
- 1 tablespoon honey or maple syrup (optional, for sweetness)
- 1/2 teaspoon vanilla extract (optional)

Instructions:

Mix Dry Ingredients:

- In a bowl, whisk together the coconut flour, baking powder, and a pinch of salt.

Combine Wet Ingredients:

- In a separate bowl, whisk the eggs. Add coconut milk, melted coconut oil or butter, honey or maple syrup (if using), and vanilla extract (if using). Mix well.

Combine Wet and Dry Mixtures:

- Pour the wet ingredients into the dry ingredients and stir until well combined. Allow the batter to sit for a few minutes to let the coconut flour absorb the liquids.

Preheat Griddle or Pan:

- Preheat a griddle or non-stick skillet over medium heat. Grease it with a little coconut oil or butter.

Scoop Batter:

- Scoop 2-3 tablespoons of batter onto the griddle for each pancake. Use the back of the spoon to spread the batter into a round shape.

Cook Until Bubbles Form:

- Cook until bubbles start to form on the surface of the pancake and the edges look set.

Flip and Cook Other Side:

- Carefully flip the pancake and cook the other side until golden brown.

Repeat:

- Repeat the process with the remaining batter, adding more oil or butter to the griddle as needed.

Serve:

- Serve the coconut flour pancakes warm with your favorite toppings, such as fresh berries, sliced bananas, or a drizzle of maple syrup.

Enjoy:

- Enjoy these delicious and fluffy coconut flour pancakes!

These pancakes are not only gluten-free but also rich in fiber and have a subtle coconut flavor. Feel free to customize the recipe by adding spices like cinnamon or nutmeg for extra flavor. They make for a delightful and wholesome breakfast or brunch option.

Sugar-Free Cheesecake Recipe

Ingredients:

For the Crust:

- 1 1/2 cups almond flour
- 1/4 cup melted butter
- 1 tablespoon sugar substitute (e.g., erythritol)

For the Filling:

- 24 ounces (3 packages) cream cheese, softened
- 1 cup sugar substitute (e.g., erythritol)
- 1 teaspoon vanilla extract
- 3 large eggs
- 1/2 cup sour cream

For Topping (Optional):

- Sugar-free fruit preserves or fresh berries

Instructions:

Preheat Oven:

- Preheat your oven to 325°F (163°C). Grease a 9-inch springform pan.

Prepare Crust:

- In a bowl, combine almond flour, melted butter, and 1 tablespoon of sugar substitute. Press the mixture into the bottom of the prepared springform pan to form the crust.

Bake Crust:

- Bake the crust in the preheated oven for about 10 minutes or until it's golden brown. Remove from the oven and let it cool while preparing the filling.

Prepare Filling:

- In a large mixing bowl, beat the softened cream cheese until smooth.
- Add 1 cup of sugar substitute and vanilla extract, and beat until well combined.
- Add the eggs one at a time, mixing well after each addition.
- Stir in the sour cream until the filling is smooth and creamy.

Pour Filling Over Crust:

- Pour the cream cheese filling over the cooled crust in the springform pan.

Bake Cheesecake:

- Bake in the preheated oven for 50-60 minutes or until the center is set and the top is lightly browned.

Cool and Chill:

- Allow the cheesecake to cool in the pan, then refrigerate for at least 4 hours or overnight for best results.

Topping (Optional):

- Before serving, you can top the cheesecake with sugar-free fruit preserves or fresh berries.

Serve:

- Slice and serve the delicious sugar-free cheesecake!

This sugar-free cheesecake offers the creamy and indulgent flavor you love without the added sugars. Feel free to experiment with different sugar substitutes and toppings to suit your taste preferences. It's a fantastic dessert for those following a low-carb or sugar-free lifestyle.

Avocado Chocolate Mousse Recipe

Ingredients:

- 2 ripe avocados, peeled and pitted
- 1/4 cup cocoa powder (unsweetened)
- 1/4 cup maple syrup or honey
- 1/4 cup milk (dairy or plant-based)
- 1 teaspoon vanilla extract
- A pinch of salt
- Optional toppings: Fresh berries, chopped nuts, or whipped cream

Instructions:

Blend Ingredients:

- In a food processor or blender, combine the ripe avocados, cocoa powder, maple syrup or honey, milk, vanilla extract, and a pinch of salt.

Blend Until Smooth:

- Blend the ingredients until the mixture is smooth and creamy. You may need to stop and scrape down the sides of the blender or food processor a few times to ensure everything is well incorporated.

Taste and Adjust:

- Taste the mousse and adjust the sweetness by adding more maple syrup or honey if desired.

Chill:

- Transfer the avocado chocolate mousse to serving bowls or glasses. Cover and refrigerate for at least 30 minutes to allow it to chill.

Serve:

- Once chilled, serve the avocado chocolate mousse with your favorite toppings, such as fresh berries, chopped nuts, or a dollop of whipped cream.

Enjoy:

- Enjoy this creamy and indulgent Avocado Chocolate Mousse as a guilt-free dessert!

This dessert is not only delicious but also loaded with the nutritional benefits of avocados. It's a great way to satisfy your chocolate cravings while incorporating the goodness of wholesome ingredients. Plus, it's vegan and gluten-free, making it suitable for various dietary preferences.

www.ingramcontent.com/pod-product-compliance
Lightning Source LLC
LaVergne TN
LVHW081550060526
838201LV00054B/1845